D1436014

Learn to Ski in a Weekend

ATOMIC
ATOMIC

LEARN TO SKI IN A WEEKEND

KONRAD BARTELSKI
with ROBIN NEILLANDS

Photography by Matthew Ward

DORLING KINDERSLEY
London • New York • Stuttgart

A DORLING KINDERSLEY BOOK

Art Editor Arthur Torr-Brown
Editor/Series Editor James Harrison

Senior Art Editor Tina Vaughan
Senior Editor Sean Moore
Production Controller Meryl Silbert

First published in Great Britain in 1991
by Dorling Kindersley Limited,
9 Henrietta Street, London WC2E 8PS
Reprinted 1993

A CIP catalogue record for this book is available from the British Library

ISBN 0-86318-662-9

Computer page make-up by The Cooling Brown Partnership
Reproduced by Colourscan, Singapore
Printed and bound in Italy by Arnoldo Mondadori, Verona.

CONTENTS

INTRODUCTION

LEARNING TO SKI IN A WEEKEND may sound like a tall order, but skiing can be a lot easier than you might suppose. This book is designed to prepare you for the challenge of sliding down a snowy slope, with a series of easy-to-follow, extremely clear, colour photographs and text, which you can first study in the comfort of your home. After reading this book you will have an understanding of the mountain environment and be aware of the particular problems that mountains can create; but you will also learn how these problems can be easily avoided or overcome. Skiing is a very simple and enjoyable sport if tackled in the correct way; you do not have to be either young or athletic to enjoy the pleasures of gliding down a slope on skis. My grandfather was 65 when he first put on a pair of skis, and many of his younger ski class mates were struggling to keep up.

Study the various sequences in *Learn to Ski in a Weekend* at home, and you will be more fluent when taking your first steps on snow. The skills I have selected will give you a solid foundation from which to gently explore the beautiful slopes and savour the excitement and atmosphere of snow and mountains. Open your eyes and absorb the beauty of what nature has to offer... you will enjoy it much more on skis.

KONRAD BARTELSKI

PREPARING FOR THE WEEKEND

Before making your first steps on snow get used to your equipment whilst learning a few basics

YOU CAN MASTER the basics of skiing on a weekend course, provided the instruction is clear and you are willing to learn. Skiing is as much a mental as a physical activity, and it will pay to prepare yourself for the weekend and ensure that your time and attention is devoted solely to the business in hand – learning the basics of skiing.

HOME PRACTICE
Getting the feel of ski equipment (pp.24-27).

Wearing in

Choose a clear weekend, free of interruptions from family, friends, or social commitments. If possible, get your equipment out on hire before your ski weekend commences, and get used to it. Handle the **poles**, wear your boots (and be sure they fit well), learn how to put on and take off your skis. All this will help to save time on the weekend itself.

Get used to the boots especially and feel comfortable wearing them. Walk around the house and get used to the extra weight they have added to the end of your legs. Walk up and down stairs in them and practise resting your weight on the edges of the boots. This will make subsequent

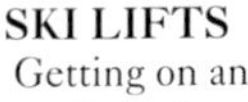

SKI LIFTS
Getting on and off tow bars (pp.14-15).

movements on skis that much more familiar. You don't need snow for any of this; the more comfortable you are with your ski equipment, the easier your skiing will be when you actually get out on the slopes.

Wearing out

Skiing is a sport and, as with all sports, it pays to be fit or, at any rate, a little fitter, before you start. This preparation should begin some weeks before the course itself, and the important element in it is to accustom your muscles to new strains and tone up the body for a certain amount of physical effort. Stretching exercises are extremely useful, as is any activity that helps to strengthen the legs.

NOTE: *Words appearing in* **bold** *are explained further in the glossary on pages* 92-93.

PUTTING ON BOOTS
Rear- and front-entry fitting (pp.18-19).

CHOOSING SKIS
Getting the right height (pp.20-21).

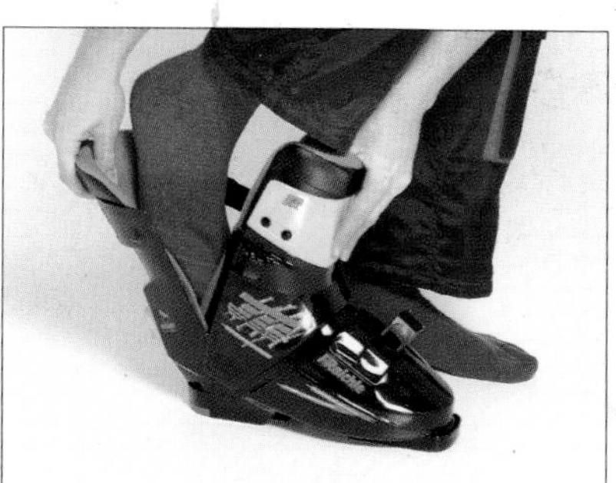

ACCLIMATIZING

Open your eyes to your new environment

ONE OF THE GREAT JOYS of skiing is that it takes place in the mountains. When you go skiing, don't let your desire to master the skills detract you from enjoying the environment, the fresh mountain air, the sunshine, and the sheer beauty of the snow-capped peaks. On a more practical point, when you arrive at the top of the **lift** and see the mountains spread out all around you, with runs

leading off in every direction, allow time for warming up, flexing your muscles, and getting your bearings. Make sure you've applied sufficient sun block and lip salve, and check that your ski **bindings** are correctly fastened, and everything is in good order before you set off. Decide where you are going and how to get there. If you don't feel confident, take a deep breath, try to relax and go back to the basics you will learn from this book. On these basic techniques rests the whole foundation of your skiing.

Above all though, remember to enjoy yourself. Skiing, and learning to ski, should be fun and will be fun if you remember to enjoy it while you are learning the techniques.

SKI RESORTS

Finding your way round a new environment

A TYPICAL SKI RESORT (below) and ski map (right), illustrating some of the sights you can expect to see, and some of the equipment you will have to use in this exhilarating environment. In the early days, most of your activity will be concentrated on the **nursery slopes**, which may not be on the lower slopes, so you may need to use a chairlift or a tow-lift before you can begin actually skiing. You will also need to carry a lift-pass. Compare the weekly ski-pass price against the day-ticket cost, before buying your ski pass.

CHAIR LIFTS
The most common ski lift (left and below), the chair lift is either a 1-, 2-, 3-, or 4-seater.

Reading the Resort Map

Ski resorts provide maps, illustrating the runs and the lifts. European resorts colour-code the runs green, blue, red, and black, in order of increasing difficulty. In the USA, a single or double black diamond is used (see pp.90-91). The types of ski lifts are shown by symbols. Always carry a map to find your way about, pick the runs that suit your level best; locate the ski school, the nursery slopes, the first-aid stations, the meeting points, and the restaurants.

Ski Map • Check carefully the mountain layout, ski runs (colour-coded for beginners, intermediates, and advanced), and the various connecting lifts.

Ski pass • A typical lift pass: day passes like this don't usually require a passport picture but weekly passes do, so be sure to take one with you. Lift passes are never cheap, so buy only for the time you need.

Map symbols • Maps have a key to the information symbols – varying from country to country, region to region, resort to resort. Always check the key and link it to the various symbols.

UP THE SLOPES

How to travel the tow-lifts

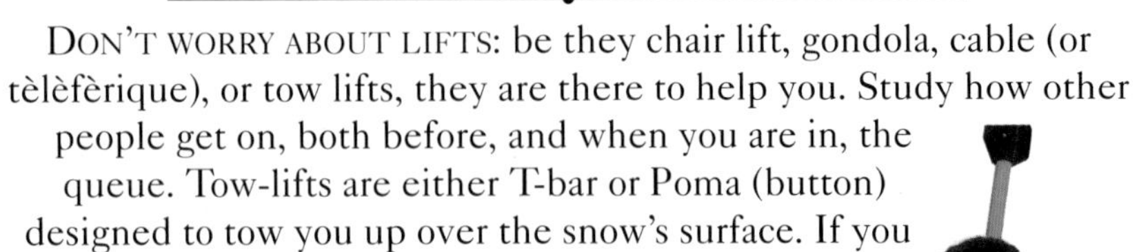

DON'T WORRY ABOUT LIFTS: be they chair lift, gondola, cable (or tèlèfèrique), or tow lifts, they are there to help you. Study how other people get on, both before, and when you are in, the queue. Tow-lifts are either T-bar or Poma (button) designed to tow you up over the snow's surface. If you drop a stick or glove, leave it, someone will bring it up.

T-BARS

Hold your **poles** in the outside hand and look round ready to take the T-bar. Two skiers stand side-by-side, turn and place the T-bar under the hips then turn to face the slope. Do not sit down.

• WATCH
Look over your shoulder and pull down the T- bar.

• GOING UP
Lean towards each other at the shoulder, and don't let your **tips** drift over the other skier's.

• THE BOTTOM LINE
Keep the skis parallel and feet apart. Do not let your boot and weight rest on the other skier. Keep the knees **flexed** but stand upright. Do not sit or rest your weight on the bar. Let it pull you along.

PULLING UP WITH A POMA

RIGHT ON THE BUTTON

Some Pomas have a very fierce pull, so as you join the queue study how these button surface-lifts work.
1 You are ready to take the Poma to put it between your legs, skis slightly apart and parallel, **poles** gripped firmly but kept out of the way. There is no need for two hands on any lift.
2 **Slide** forward into position, skis parallel, keeping the poles in the outer hand, and take the Poma in the other hand; put it between your legs. Keep the knees bent and prepare for the jerk as the cable unwinds. Many skiers fall off at this point because they are unprepared for the jerk.

LETTING GO Let go gently – so the bar does not spring wildly in the air – but not too soon.

LOOK Watch out for skiers in front of you.

SAFE RELEASE

Don't get off too soon. Wait at the top of the slope until the ground slopes away before you. The second skier does not release the T-bar until it is safe to do so (the first skier off, skis out of the way). Pull the T-bar away from your body and let it go. Never loiter in the path of other skiers.

TIMING Don't release yourself while you are still coming up the hill. Wait for the crest.

PREPARING Prepare to get off 50m (about 55yd) from the end of the run. On the T-bar, agree who will get off first.

CLOTHING

Layers are the key to keeping warm in near-zero temperatures

WHATEVER STYLE of ski gear you go for, remember to wear ski clothing in layers. Air trapped between the layers of clothing will provide the necessary insulation against the elements. Make sure your ski clothing is warm, windproof, and, ideally, waterproof, and also made of breathable fabric to help control perspiration levels.

SUNGLASSES •
Sunglasses protect eyes from strong glare, improve visibility in poor weather conditions, and should provide protection from the strong ultra-violet light. Polarized lenses are best for cutting out glare; plastic is safer in case of falls.

• PROTECTION
Apply a high-factor sunscreen regularly to block out powerful ultraviolet rays and a lip-salve to avoid chapped lips from the wind chill.

• CORD
Attach a bright cord to your ski glasses to avoid loss.

JACKET •
The ski jacket should be wind- and waterproof. Look for strong zips covered with flaps and drawstrings for extra insulation. Check the manufacturer's details for fabric material etc..

GLOVES •
Choose gloves that are large enough to permit free movement of the fingers and thick enough to keep the fingers warm. See that the cuffs extend over the wrists and the palms are reinforced.

GOGGLES •
Goggles provide wider eye-area protection against cold, driving snow, or very strong sunlight. Keep them in your jacket when not in use to protect them against scratches and to avoid losing them.

SOCKS •
With modern boots, only one pair of socks is necessary. Buy ski socks which are long, warm, of a wool and fibre mix, and of loop-stitch construction. They should fit snugly to prevent blisters.

• SALOPETTES

Be sure the fit is comfortable at the shoulders (with adjustable straps) and crotch, even when you bend over – and that the waist is high on the back.

• ONE-PIECE SUITS

These are very warm, snug, and smart. They can even be too hot when the sun is out, so be sure that you can fold down the top and tie the arms around the waist.

COLOUR SENSE

Choose colourful clothing for added visibility, and to help avoid accidents.

THERMALS •

Thermal underwear is an essential element in layer clothing. Two-piece outfits are more convenient than a single garment – very effective when worn with a one-piece ski-suit.

EXTREME PROTECTION

Dressing in layers keeps the body warm, but be sure to protect the extremities – the ears, toes, fingers, and wrists, where the blood runs closest to the skin. Mittens are warmer than gloves. Hats must cover the ears.

Headband

Goggles

Glove

Mitten

Inner glove

Woollen hat

SKI BOOTS

The vital link between you and your skis, ski boots can make or break your skiing

APART FROM their technical role in attaching the skier to the ski, and inducing the correct forward lean, ski boots must feel comfortable. Badly fitting boots have driven more first-time skiers from the ski slopes than anything else. Don't make a spur-of-the-moment decision: listen to expert advice at a ski shop and try on many pairs.

REAR-ENTRY BOOTS

The popular rear-entry ski boot has a hinged flap behind the ankle which drops back to let the foot in, and when shut pushes the foot forward into the correct position.

INNER BOOT • Padded to keep the foot warm and insulated, it should fill the boot completely, protecting the ankles and the toes from chafing.

• **REAR FASTENER** Look for adjustable clips that, while securing the foot, do not push the toes hard against the front of the boot.

• **FOREFOOT ADJUSTMENT** Many types of rear- entry boot are adjusted by means of a fastener on the front. Check this fastener enables you to tighten the boot adequately without pinching or hurting the foot.

—*FEELING FOR FIT*—

Ski boots require adjustment to maintain the correct fit throughout the day. Make sure that the toes are not pressed tightly against the front of the boot, and that the heel of the foot is kept down. When strapping on your boot, keep your heel down, while your ankle must be free to bend, allowing you to rock into the **forward lean** position. Your shin should rest against the padded tongue of the boot and the bend of the ankle must coincide with the hinge point. There should be just enough room to wiggle your toes. Remember: a boot that fits well is a comfortable boot.

INTO A REAR-ENTRY BOOT

THE INS AND OUTS

Any ski boot has two basic elements: the padded inner boot for comfort and **flex,** and the outer shell or chassis, to support your natural ski movements. The shell and inner boot combine to keep the foot firm and the heel down. During each day's skiing your foot warms up, so you need to adjust the fit as the padding settles down and the boot loosens. With rear-entry boots the fit is tightened or relaxed by altering the inner boot, which you can do from the outside by turning catches to tighten an internal cable.

PUTTING ON BOOTS

First open the boot up completely. Now smooth the socks to take out any wrinkles. Slide the foot in and do up the boot until the fit is comfortable. The fit must be firm but flexible, and not tight.

Inner boot

Heel retention adjuster

Heel retention strap

Inner sole

Forefoot adjuster

INNER BOOT
Slipping in and out of the inner boot should be an effortless action. If it isn't, try another boot.

ANKLE SUPPORT
The boot must hold the ankle firmly, gripping the heel lightly on either side of the main tendon.

FLEX
Even with the clips fastened, you must be able to **flex** at the ankle when adopting a **forward lean** position.

FRONT-ENTRY BOOT

Put on front-entry boots like normal shoes. Adjust them throughout the day by moving wires, on clips on the shell, up and down a grooved ratchet. To improve **forward lean** and achieve the desired skiing posture, many skiers leave the upper clips quite loose. If you do this, take a firmer grip on the ankle bend clip, to hold the heel down.

TOE-PIECE
The boot is attached to the toe binding by the toe-piece. Get worn edges checked at a ski shop.

SKIS AND POLES

Selecting and safeguarding your skis and poles

THE BASIC AIM of all ski equipment is to make skiing easier – whatever the prevailing fashion. When hiring or buying ski equipment, make sure the **bindings** are not loose or badly fitted, and that the skis are sharp, with complete **edges,** and bases free from scars. Poles must have complete baskets and secure straps.

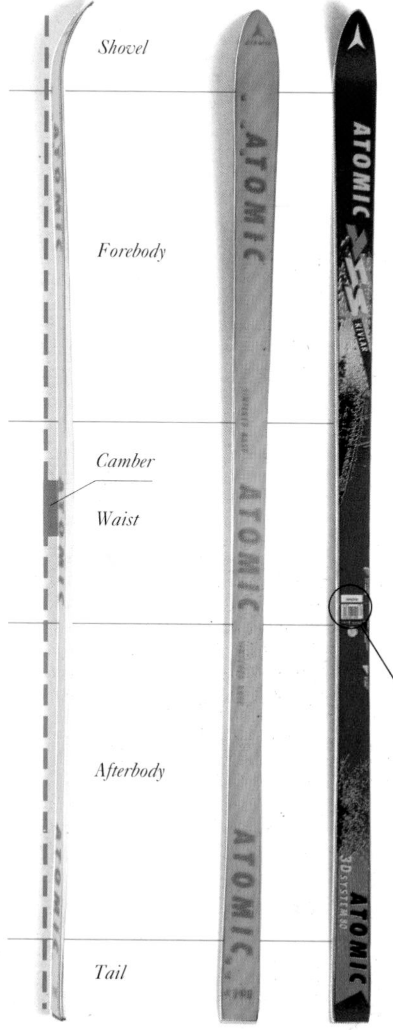

SELECTING SKIS

When buying or hiring check that the ski is not warped in any way, and that the running base is smooth and flat. The ski should be fairly flexible at the **tip** but spring back into position when released. The geometry of modern skis remains relatively unchanged, but the materials have changed radically.

SHOVEL

The shovel plays a major role in the turning process, as it **flexes** and leads the skier round.

WAIST

The narrowest point of the ski, the **waist** is where you place your boot. The ski is arched, or has **camber,** to support your weight, and to control the various forces put on it.

TAIL

Without a skier, the ski would only touch the snow at two points – the shovel and **tail.** The tail is tipped up to reduce possible abrasion.

SELECTION SYMBOLS

International symbols engraved on the **waist** help you choose skis according to height, weight, and experience – "L" for beginner, "A" for intermediate (as seen here), "S" for expert etc. Get advice at the ski shop.

Advanced

Beginner

FINDING THE RIGHT LENGTH

Use your height (see left) as a yardstick for the length of ski you need. As a rough guide: beginner is head height, intermediate 10-15cm (4-6in) above head height, and advanced 15-30cm (6-12in) above head height. Weight, fitness, and previous experience also affect your choice of ski length and design.

SKI POLES

Designed as much for balance as for helping you to turn, **ski poles** must be the correct length, making your forearms form a natural horizontal. So, when holding the poles, check that your elbows form a 90° angle.

ARMS • Note the correct position of the arm, parallel to the ground, bent at right angles from the elbow. This is not possible if the pole is too long or short.

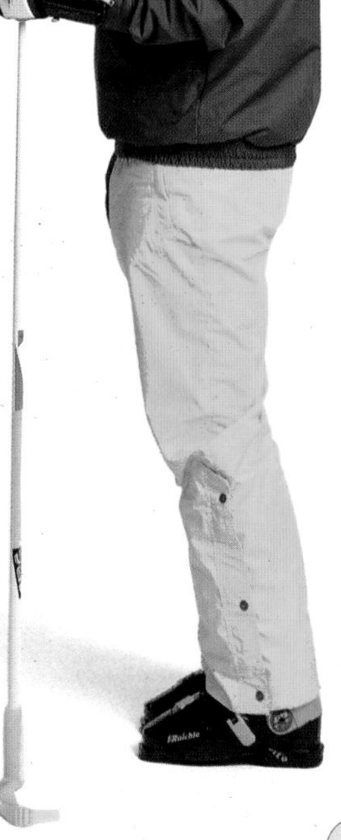

LOCKING BASKETS

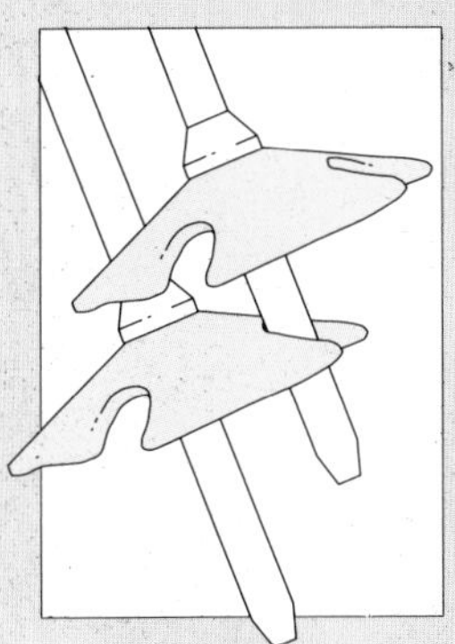

BASKETS
Plastic baskets usually have one hole cut in them, so you can put the tip of one **ski pole** through the basket hole of the other and clip them together for carrying. Baskets prevent the pole from vanishing into the snow. Lost baskets should be replaced as soon as you possibly can.

SKI BINDINGS

The anchor for all your ski activities

SKI BINDINGS – the most complicated item of your ski equipment – are a mechanism that have the dual function of holding the boot firmly to the ski, yet releasing under pressure. If your bindings are not correctly adjusted, you will either find your skis coming off at the wrong time, or failing to come off when they should, which could lead to an accident. Well-adjusted bindings are essential, and they should be adjusted only by a qualified ski mechanic.

SECURING PIECE

The **binding** has two main parts: a toe-piece and heel-piece. Though it can vary, the toe-piece normally releases under sideways pressure and the heel-piece under forward and upward pressure. Some bindings have a heel pivot, so the whole heel binding swivels to release the boot.

HEEL-PIECE
The heel-piece also has a setting indicator. Have the adjustment checked by an authorized ski shop.

SKI STOPPERS
Two prongs that project down when your ski comes off, and stop it sliding away.

TOE PIECE
The toe-piece is a spring-loaded mechanism, designed to release your ski boot when the forces on your leg build up to a dangerous level. The setting indicator shows the tightness of the **binding** on the boot, and should be pre-set in an authorized ski shop.

GETTING RELEASED
Before you get into the **bindings** find out how to release them. Many bindings, like the ones shown here, are released by pushing down on a latch with the **ski pole**.

BOUND AND RELEASED

UNDER PRESSURE

Locate the toe of your boot into the **binding** between the toe-piece and the heel-piece. The heel-piece is spring-loaded, and the spring can be tightened or released so that the binding is correctly adjusted to that point where it will release under the right pressure. There is, however, another advantage in a well-adjusted binding, for this will also offer a degree of "give", or elasticity, in the binding, to absorb the bumps and shock of normal skiing without release.

A binding that comes off too easily or too suddenly is as dangerous as one which refuses to release under pressure. Good, well-maintained and correctly adjusted bindings are vital for your skiing safety. Have the binding fitted and adjusted by a competent ski mechanic at a ski shop.

Heel-piece – upward release

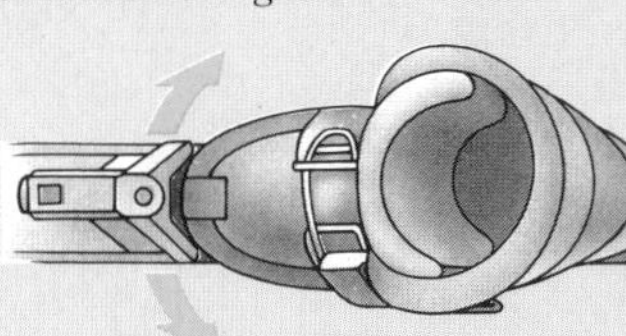

Toe-piece – sideways release

LATERAL RELEASE

All bindings can release laterally, but some release vertically at the toe-piece.

HEEL RELEASE MECHANISM

The most important elements of your heel-piece are the setting indicator, the adjustment screw, and the manual release. Check also that the ski brake (or stopper) is working.

BINDING RELEASE
Check that you know how to get your boot out of the **binding.** The release is always from the heel-piece, usually with the aid of a **ski-pole** pressing down on a latch, or by treading on the back of the binding.

Brake plate

SETTING INDICATOR
A graduated scale indicates the best setting for your particular boot. Make a mental note of the setting so that you can, if necessary, adjust the **binding** for yourself should it become loose.

ADJUSTMENT SCREW
This varies the setting of the **binding**, and should only be adjusted by a qualified technician.

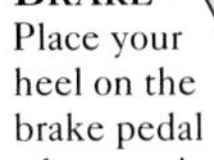

BRAKE
Place your heel on the brake pedal when getting on the **binding,** and the brake prongs will rise.

Forward pressure adjustment screw

GETTING THE FEEL

Learning to move naturally in ski gear

YOU CAN ACCELERATE the learning process greatly if you wear your ski gear before the weekend commences, and get used to moving about – particularly in ski boots and while handling **ski poles**. This also gets the muscles used to some of the basic skiing stances.

ADAPTING TO BOOTS

Walk up and down the stairs at home in ski boots, and get your body adapting naturally to the feel of moving in them, and to the restrictions of shape and size. Further in-house exercises enable you to practise other skiing skills like **edging** and **side-stepping** – see opposite.

HEAD
Good skiing posture means head up and eyes forward to take in as wide a view as possible. Feel the position, don't look for it.

BODY
Keep your upper body relaxed and leaning slightly forward in the position you'll need for skiing down a slope.

BALANCE
Keep your balance central over the ball of your foot. Do not creep downstairs in a "sit-down" position.

ARMS
Using the banisters to guide you, the arms naturally take up the slightly forward, slightly bent position. Keep your hands forward of the body.

LEGS
Keep your weight on the rear leg, which supports your body and keeps it balanced, while the other leg goes down a next step.

KNEES/FEET
Flex the upper knee so the lower leg goes forward and down, with feet slightly apart. Be careful or you may trip up.

—USING A MIRROR IMAGE—

MEMORIZING THE FEEL

A mirror is a useful training aid for checking your posture and position. Many skiers are horrified when they see a photograph or a video film and realize how poor their posture is. Study the skills shown in this book and then practise the positions with the aid of a mirror.

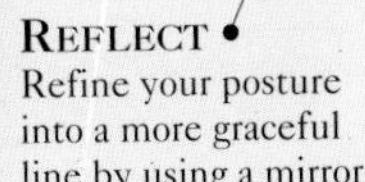

REFLECT •
Refine your posture into a more graceful line by using a mirror.

SIDE-STEPPING

Duplicate the **side-stepping** action (see pp.42-43) at home without the encumbrance of skis. Do not stand on the edge of your boots. Just be sure to shift your weight firmly from one boot to the other as you climb up and down.

POLE PRACTISING

To get the feel of climbing and descending slopes, practise with poles or the substitutes shown here. Climbing up, move the upper pole, then the upper leg, then the lower leg, then the lower pole, 1-2-3-4, in co-ordinated movements.

UPPER BODY •
Keep the upper body relaxed, leaning slightly forward, weight over the hips, looking across the stairs and not down at your feet. Stay in balance and **transfer** your **weight** firmly without swaying about. Use the "poles" for balance.

FEET •
Keep your feet flat on the floor. Do not rock onto your toes or heels, or sideways on the boot. **Flex** the ankle well forward against the front of the boot.

PRE-SKI PRACTISING

Go outdoors and play in your ski clothes and boots, practising the skiing positions shown here in your garden or in the local park. It all serves to reduce the learning time when you get on the slope. **Edging** on a slope makes you adopt this position to stay up-right.

HEAD
Look forward, not down. Keep your eyes focused on the direction you would be going.

ARMS
Bend the arms slightly to one side in a "half-hoop" position. Imagine you are holding ski poles.

BALANCE
Feet and ankles take up correct **traverse**.

FEET
In the **traverse**, the position of the feet is critical. Turn the feet and ankles so that you **edge** into the slope and get grip. When you add skis and snow it will come to feel as natural as with trainers on grass.

STANDING ON A SLOPE
Learning to stand sideways on a slope teaches how to adjust your position and **edge** your feet into the slope. Adopt the **comma** position (see pp.60-61) and use it to maintain balance and grip on a slope.

GETTING THE EDGING FEELING

EDGING ALONG
Edging is one of the most useful basic skills. Remember that the **edges** of your skis provide the grip in the **traverse** and act as brakes when you are moving. They provide a large part of the control and, in the traverse, are the only way you can maintain your position on the slope, and head safely and evenly in the direction you wish to go. The two vital ingredients needed to get a good grip with both ski edges are the angle of the boots and skis, together with the use of your weight.

Edge the skis in order to provide an adequate amount of grip into the slope, and increase the amount of edging as the angle of the slope increases. Practise this by moving your knees and ankles into the slope, turning your trainers or ski boots right onto their edges, almost fully exposing the soles. To compensate for this movement shift the upper body out over the slope. The steeper the slope, the more you need to lean out. You may find it difficult at first, but this is the most secure position. Don't lean into the slope.

THE FITNESS FACTOR

BENDING AND STRETCHING

Skiing is a sport. It can be practised at a wide range of levels, but it remains a sport. You will enjoy it more, get more out of it, and be far less tired at the end of the day, if you get a little fitter before heading for the slopes. A number of other sports are particularly useful because they employ the same muscles, require the same kind of energy release employed in skiing, or provide useful practise in co-ordinated movements. Skiing exercises the body mainly by bending, stretching, turning, and adjusting. There is little need for hard physical effort, but the leg muscles do take a lot of pounding, and people who come totally unfit to the snow slopes will find skiing quite hard work.

CO-ORDINATION AND WEIGHT TRANSFERENCE

Tennis requires hand-eye and leg co-ordination, balance, poise, and weight transference – qualities that are equally useful in skiing – besides exercising a wide range of muscles (see below).

KNEES Weight shifted over bent forward knee. **Transfering weight** from one foot to the other is a basic skiing skill.

PEDAL PRESSURE

Pedalling on a bicycle produces a similar reaction in the leg muscles to that needed for a ski turn, as pressure is taken off one leg and placed on the other to initiate a turn.

BALANCE Skiing, like tennis and cycling, calls for a sound moving platform.

LEG STRETCHING Cycling exercises the long muscles in the lower leg and thighs, compressing them as for a ski turn and stretching them again on the full extent of the pedal, or for a downhill run - a **schuss**.

THE WEEKEND COURSE

Grasping the course at a glance

WELCOME TO OUR WEEKEND ski course. Practise the 14 skills covered here, and you will finish the weekend with a good grasp of the basic techniques and – equally important – confidence in your ability to absorb more skiing at a faster pace as your confidence increases. The course not only teaches skills, but also tackles and eliminates common problems that affect skiers early on, and prevent them making rapid and enjoyable progress. The emphasis throughout is on getting the basics right with constant practice, stressing the importance of a good posture, natural balance, and the belief that when it feels right, it is right.

DAY 1		*Hours*	*Page*
SKILL 1	Getting ready	1/2	30-33
SKILL 2	Moving around	1/2	34-35
SKILL 3	Falling down	1/2	36-39
SKILL 4	Getting up	1/2	40-41
SKILL 5	Side-stepping	1/2	42-43
SKILL 6	Changing direction	1	44-47
SKILL 7	Snow Plough	1 1/2	48-51
SKILL 8	Schussing	1	52-53

Changing direction (p.46)

Snow plough (p.49)

KEY TO SYMBOLS

CLOCKS

On the first page of each new skill, a small clock designates, through the blue-coloured section, how much time you might give to the skill, and how this fits in to your overall course. So the blue segment on p.54 shows you a recommended 2 hours on snow-plough turns. But remember to be flexible and to use the clocks as guidelines only. Every learner will find their own natural pace for learning skiing skills.

RATING SYSTEM •••••

Each skill is given a rating according to the degree of difficulty. One point (•) denotes that the skill is comparatively easy, while 5 points (•••••) shows a much more challenging skill.

MICRO-SKIERS

The micro-skiers alongside most skills, help you identify the key steps or stages assigned to that technique. The blue micro-skiers link to the photographic steps.

ARROWS

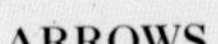

The blue dotted arrow indicates the **fall line,** the steepest path down the slope; the red arrow accentuates the **weighting/unweighting** process, and the blue arrow highlights general body movement.

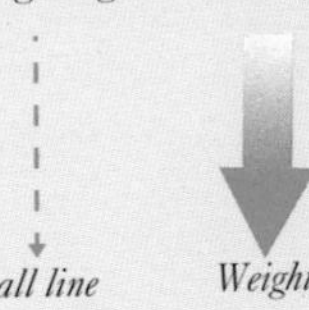

Fall line *Weight* *Body movement*

DAY 2	Hours	Page
SKILL 9 Snow-plough turn	2	54-59
SKILL 10 Traversing	1/2	60-61
SKILL 11 Timing	1	62-65
SKILL 12 Side-slipping	1	66-69
SKILL 13 Reading the slope	1	70-75
SKILL 14 Fine tuning	1/2	76-79

Side-slipping (p.69)

Snow-plough turn (p.55)

Advanced snow-plough stop (p.79)

SKILL

DAY 1

1 GETTING READY

Definition: *To carry and put on skis; to find a natural ski posture*

BEFORE YOU PUT SKI to slope, you first need to get to the slope, properly clad and fully equipped; and at the same time become mentally prepared for learning a new set of skills in an unfamiliar and unpredictable environment. Allow time to feel familiar with the skis on a flat surface. Relax and stay calm.

OBJECTIVE: To avoid early mistakes, allowing time to acclimatize yourself on skis. *Rating* ••

CARRYING SKIS

Lock your skis together and then balance them over your shoulder, just in front of the **bindings.** Keep the **tips** down looping an arm over the skis just behind the tips. Keep **tails** clear of people's heads.

Use poles as a walking stick

—*LINKING YOUR SKI STOPPERS*—

LOCK-TIGHT

Ski brakes, or stoppers, are designed to prevent the ski from running away after a fall, or if you take it off on a slope. Use them also to clamp the skis together for carrying.

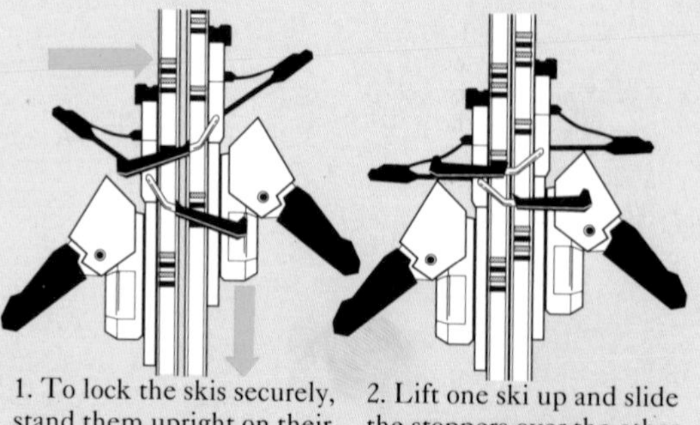

1. To lock the skis securely, stand them upright on their tails, back-to-back.

2. Lift one ski up and slide the stoppers over the other, letting it drop and link up.

PUTTING ON SKIS

Check your **bindings:** see that the heel is open. Now clean the snow off the underside of your boots, preferably by scraping with a **ski pole,** or with the other boot. Try to find a flat spot to put your skis on. But if you find yourself on a slope, always put your lowest ski on first so you can **edge** in to the slope for grip.

1. Lay the skis down and then firmly tap the snow from the boot with your pole.

2. Fit one boot in to the binding and stamp down hard to secure.

3. Tap snow from second boot. Keep balance with the poles and put on second ski.

SKI STANCE

Though not a natural posture, the classic ski stance should come to you naturally as you **flex** and adjust your body. The **forward lean** of the ski boot and length of **ski pole** will ease you into the posture. Pre-ski practise (see pp.26-29) will also help you find your natural balance and weight distribution over the skis.

HEAD
Hold your head up, eyes in front and neck relaxed. Don't look down at the **tips.**

ARMS
Relax the arms just forward of the hips and **flex** elbows slightly. Avoid stiff arms beside or behind the body.

BODY
Upper body upright with hips eased forward to put the weight over the balls of the feet. Avoid sticking your backside out.

SKIS
Keep the skis flat and parallel on the snow, and avoid overlapping

LOWER BODY
Relax the legs and bend the knees so that they **flex** over the toe cap of the boot. Flex the ankles forward to allow the shin to rest against the tongue of the boot. Make sure the feet are slightly apart, supporting your relaxed "hung over" bodyweight evenly.

SKILL

1

Getting Used to Skis

Practise **transferring** the **weight** from one ski to the other and adjusting your balance, stabilizing yourself meanwhile with your **poles.** At first it may feel strange to move around on skis, but with a little practice it becomes much easier, and you soon learn to allow for the extra length the ski adds to your foot.

Leg Lift the leg up until the knee is well bent, allowing the ankle to **flex** down so the ski **tip** rests on the surface.

LIFTING

Lift the ski up, leaving the **tip** of the ski on the ground. All your weight is now down on the lower ski and you must remain in balance before putting the ski down, **transferring** the **weight** to it and lifting the other ski in the same fashion.

Pole Maintain balance with your **ski poles.**

Tips Note the **tip** of the upper ski touches the ground.

GETTING TO GRIPS

A firm grip of your **ski poles** is an aid to positive skiing. It is also important to put on the pole strap in the correct manner. Straps should not be allowed to dangle limply from your wrist. The strap stops your pole from sliding off downhill if you fall and let go of it, so observe the following instructions closely.

1 Shake the pole strap free, and put your hand in from below.

2 Make sure the strap lies over the back of the hand, just behind the thumb.

3 Pull down on the strap, so that it becomes tight across the back of the hand.

—*EDGING PRACTICE*—

Practise rocking onto the **edge** of your skis, as shown below. Note the position of the **poles** and the fact that the body is well balanced over the skis. Continue this exercise by putting all the weight on one **edged** ski, and lifting the other clear of the surface.

REVERSE CAMBER
The ski arches with its entire inside **edge** biting into the slope.

SHUFFLING

A shuffling exercise has two purposes; firstly it warms up and stretches leg muscles and gets them ready for skiing. Secondly, it helps you improve your ability in **transferring** the **weight** from one ski to the other. Study the skier below and note that when the weight is on the right ski, the left ski slides freely to and fro. Repeat this exercise, changing the weight from ski to ski. The weight is always on the forward leg, and the body is kept forward and over it throughout the exercise.

ARMS
Keep the arms away from the body, bent at the elbows. Some of your weight rests in the straps of the **poles.**

BODY
Keep the body forward over the front leg. Balance is maintained by the ski **poles** and by placing the weight over the forward leg.

WEIGHT TRANSFER
Practise **weight transference** from one leg to the other as the ski slides forward, leaving the unweighted ski free to move. Your ski posture does not change.

LEG
Push the ski back until the rear leg is straight, keeping the front leg bent as shown.

Slide to and fro transferring weight smoothly

SKIS
Note the skis are slightly **edged,** to maintain a grip on any slight slope.

SKILL

2 MOVING AROUND

DAY 1

Definition: *To walk, glide, and slide on level ground*

YOUR FIRST ATTEMPTS to move on skis are likely to produce your first fall. Moving around on skis takes practice, but you need to be able to walk on skis and **slide** along the flat with the minimum of effort, and to get used to the feel of the equipment.

OBJECTIVE: To get the natural feel of being on skis. *Rating* •••

WALKING

Try to keep the movement as close as possible to ordinary walking, moving each arm with the opposite leg, and **sliding** the ski forward over the snow without lifting the foot too high. Be careful not to tread on the pole basket or trip over your skis. Above all, don't try to go too fast.

HEAD
Look up and forward, not down at your skis. Note your arm and leg movements and try to keep them co-ordinated.

ARMS
Swing each arm forward in turn, keeping the elbow bent and **plant** the **pole** firmly in the snow to assist balance. Do not over-reach your arm or you may fall.

SKIS
Keep the skis on the snow – parallel and comfortably apart, so you won't trip over the **tip** or tread on the **tail**.

LEGS
Take short strides, keeping the knees bent and the weight evenly distributed, **sliding** it forward onto the leading ski as you advance. It will help to loosen the top clips of the boot, which allows the ankle to bend freely.

CHECKLIST

DO'S AND DON'TS

- Do not look at skis.
- Avoid tension in the neck and shoulders.
- Do not over-reach; no exaggerated movements.
- Arms bent and swung rhythmically.
- Keep the knees bent and the weight evenly distributed over both skis.
- Keep the skis parallel and on the snow.
- Slide the skis along, don't step.
- Keep your gliding motion rhythmical.
- Don't rely on arm strength to push.

GLIDING

Skis are designed to glide and will do so if you employ the **double-pole push** on sloping terrain. Reach out with the arms bent and **plant** both **poles** together, then lean forward, putting the weight on the poles and push yourself forward. Allow the poles to drift behind you as you **slide** between them, and bring the arms forward.

DOUBLE POLE PUSH
Allow the body to sink down so that your weight falls on the **poles,** causing them (not the strength of your arms) to push you forward.

HEAD
Eyes look forward and neck relaxed. Do not look down at your feet or ski **tips.**

ARMS
When **pole planting,** keep the arms bent and plant slightly inclined to the rear, not vertically. Relax your arms in the swing, stiffening them only when pole planting.

ARMS
Keep the arms bent – not thrust out to their full extent, but stiff enough at the elbow to **transfer** the **weight** from your body to the **poles.**

LEGS
Flex the legs and keep them slightly apart (ensuring the knees, as always, are over the toe of the boot), so evenly distributing your weight.

SKILL

DAY 1

3 FALLING DOWN

Definition: *Falling down is part of the ski-learning process*

EVERYBODY FALLS: first-time skiers, Olympic competitors, World Cup racers. Don't worry about it. Falls rarely hurt or cause injury, but you need to learn the technique early on, because falling down (and getting up) can be very tiring if you don't do it properly. Aim to control your fall: this facilitates the getting up process.

OBJECTIVE: To learn the safest and easiest way to fall. *Rating* •••••

Step 3

CHOOSE A SPOT

Let it happen, but choose your spot; take evasive action to avoid ice or rock or other skiers. Let your back-side go first.

ARMS Spread the arms wide to keep them out of the way.

KNEES Relax the legs and knees and let your backside take the strain. You must not land on your knees or elbows, as these joints are easily damaged or wrenched.

TRUNK Turn the body to present the maximum surface to the snow when you fall. Keep the **poles** clear of the body.

LEGS Let the legs relax and keep your feet together if you can, when you have touched the snow.

SKIS Fall with the skis across the **fall line**, turning the inner **edges** in to bite into the snow and improve their braking action.

KEEPING ACROSS THE FALL LINE

THE RIGHT ANGLE

As the **fall line** is the steepest line down the slope, make sure you fall across this line – to prevent your skis simply pulling you further down in the fastest, least controlled way. Try also to **edge** your skis at right angles to the snow. The edges act as brakes (see p.51). Now the fall may be over, but don't be in too much of a hurry to get up. Relax, then clear the snow away from your glasses or goggles, check your skis, **bindings,** and **poles,** and make sure that your skis are across the **fall line.**

LEG MUSCLES

Draw up your legs like this, to act as a springboard for getting up. Keep the skis across the **fall line**, with the uphill edges cutting into the snow, or you will start to slide again as you rise.

Fall line

Step 4

SIT DOWN

Aim, if you can, to get your backside on the uphill side of the slope. Don't sit down on your ski **tails** or you simply toboggan on across the slope, out of control. Try to **slide** into the fall, rather than sitting down heavily and abruptly.

ARMS

Spread the arms to keep the **poles** away from the body and stop you rolling down the slope.

POLES

Keep **poles** away from the body. You will need them to get up, so do not let them become trapped underneath you.

BODY

Rest the body on the back and the hips, with knees bent away from snow, and wrists and elbows, out of the way. Try to take the fall on the softest part of your body.

Fall line

SKILL

3

CONTROLLED FALLING

The falling sequence (running from top right, opposite page to below left) demonstrates the objective of falling safely, cushioning the impact on the fleshy parts of the body rather than on the joints, and ending up in a position from which it is easy to rise again. Remember that fast falls tend to do less harm than slow ones, but wherever possible pick your spot, and aim to get your bottom down first.

FAULTFINDER

USING POLES TO STOP
Don't jab your **poles** into the snow. You may injure your wrist and take a nasty twisting fall. Keep the poles behind you.

FALLING ON YOUR HANDS
Avoid falling on hands, as your arms are weaker than your legs. If you fall forward, try to roll over onto your side.

LEGS
Keep the legs bent and the knees clear of the snow. Tuck the feet back under the thighs or hips, not straight out. In this position they will help you regain your balance.

SKIS
Angle the skis across the **fall line** and keep them **edged.** The edges are your brakes, and this position prevents the skis **sliding** away halfway through getting up.

RELAX

The sudden realization of an impending fall may be frightening, but try to relax. Snow is soft. Look ahead and pick a spot. Do not fight the fall but try to control it.

SIT DOWN
Start to turn the skis and **edge** them, sitting down and swinging the hips towards the snow. This will reduce speed and lessen the impact. Keep the ski **poles** wide and avoid sitting down on poles or skis.

ARMS
Hold the arms wide and straight, as well as flat, to reduce the chance of tumbling, and keep the **poles** clear of the body.

BODY
Let the body **flex** and bend. Do not stiffen, but sit down to reduce your height and the distance from the snow.

BODY TWIST
With the skis now across the **fall line**, twist the body to turn the knees away from the slope and the point of impact, and turn your hips and body into the slope. Let your knees bend all the time.

Fall line

FEAR OF FALLING

EVERY SKIER FALLS

• Falling is part of skiing: don't be afraid of falling. Remember to choose where you fall and initiate the falling procedure outlined above to minimize the impact and ensure you finish the fall ready and able to get up again.

• If your skis come off you will need to find them and clean the snow from the **binding** and the boot before putting them on again (see p.31).

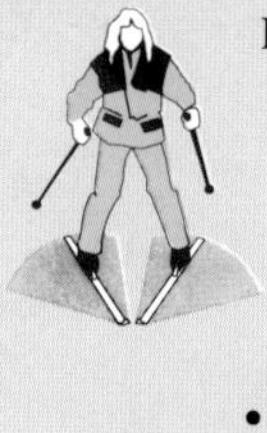

BREAKING YOUR FALL

• Easier said than done; try to avoid falling on ice and rock, otherwise do not resist the inevitable fall. Be careful particularly not to land on your knees, wrists or elbows.

• Fall across the **fall line**, that is the most direct line down the slope. The fall line provides your skis with an axis of resistance against a further **slide,** and a secure base from which to rise again.

SKILL

4 GETTING UP

DAY 1

Definition: *Rising after a fall with minimum effort*

YOU'VE LEARNED HOW to fall, ready to rise again; now learn to rise while avoiding another fall. Get your breath back, clear away the snow, put your skis back on (see pp.31, 37) if necessary. Then relax and compose yourself. Remember to use the **fall line**.

OBJECTIVE: To shift you up safely. *Rating* ••••

• **ARMS**
Straighten the arms close to the side of the head. Don't rest them on top of the **poles;** support them firmly by placing hands in the straps.

Step 1

PLACING POLES

The skier (left) sits up, knees bent, skis **edged,** well poised for getting up. **Plant** the **poles** beside the body at full arm's stretch. The rising effort comes from the legs rather than from the arms, for the legs are stronger and this is far less tiring.

• **SKIS**
Draw up the skis close to the hips, slightly apart and **edged** into the snow across the **fall line.** Put most of your weight on the lowest ski.

POLES TOGETHER

USING BOTH POLES TO PUSH UP

On a steep slope and on hard-packed snow, it is easy to get up using both **poles** for support while the skis are braced across the **fall line.**

1 Remove the hands from the ski straps and put the poles together.
2 **Plant** the **poles** in the snow above the hips, one hand near the basket and the other through the straps.
3 With the legs now drawn up, all you do is push down hard with the knees, and push lightly away with the poles. You will rise at an angle from the snow, balanced by the poles, supported by the legs, and secured by the skis across the fall line.

A HELPING HAND

BEING HELPED UP

A helping hand is always welcome, especially in deep snow where it is hard to get a firm foot- or hand-hold. Make sure you both have your skis across the **fall line** if you are on a slope. Even on a flat **piste**, as with the two skiers (right), your skis can run away with you once you get up, so **edge** your skis into the snow. Grasp the support skier's wrist, providing a double grip. The effort of rising is taken largely on your legs (keep bending the legs and avoid any straightening from the hips) with the support skier providing the balance. Keep your body bent and your weight balanced as you rise, or you will **slide** away and both may end up in a heap.

Step 2

PUSHING UP

You rise by pushing up with the legs while keeping the skis **edged.** Don't let the body fall back. Push forward on the **poles** so that, as you regain the vertical, your weight is evenly balanced over the skis, which should be kept edged at all times. Remember: use the legs, stay balanced, keep the skis edged.

• **GRIP**
Turn the wrists to bring the back of the hands forward, keeping the elbows down and the hands at about shoulder height.

SKILL 5

DAY 1

Side-Stepping

Definition: *Gaining height while maintaining direction*

The most efficient way of climbing up a steeper slope, and one that you will use every day to move up and down across the **fall line;** the **side-step** helps you to gain height and find the best position to start your run.

OBJECTIVE: To climb up and down the slope safely on skis. *Rating* ••••

Head Keep looking straight ahead or down the slope. Do not look up the slope. You must be able to feel the position of your skis across the **fall line** without looking at them.

Upper Body Keep the upper body bent just slightly forward, putting a little weight on the **poles**.

Knees Keep your knees slightly bent and turned into the slope for better **edging.**

Basic Position

This is where practising the position in front of a mirror, or on the stairs at home before you go skiing, will stand you in good stead (see p.27). The secret of **side-stepping** is balance and keeping the ski **edges** across the **fall line.**

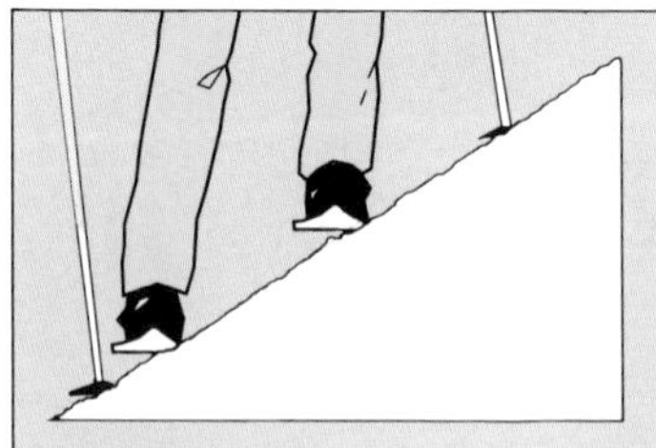

EDGE YOUR SKIS
The **edges** of the skis provide the grip. The steeper the slope the more you must edge the skis.

Steps 1 - 3

STEP-BY-STEP

The secret of successful **side-stepping** is an even change of weight from one ski to the other. Keep the skis across the **fall line**. Never move more than one arm or leg at a time, and maintain the correct ski posture. You can also use the side-step for getting down the slope as well as up it.

Remember, your skis must be across the fall line at all times.

ARMS
Keep the arms away from the body for better balance, and to avoid stepping on the **pole** basket at the end of a step.

BODY WEIGHT
When standing still, hold the weight on the downhill ski. To move uphill, move the upper ski, **transfer** the **weight** to it firmly, and step up, transferring the weight to the downhill ski again ready for the next step up. Reverse this process for stepping downhill.

BALANCE
Do not try to go too fast. Stay in balance, moving your weight smoothly from one ski to the other and using the **poles** to maintain your position.

WEIGHT TRANSFER
See the **weight transfer** from the lower to the upper ski, but still in balance. Do not let the upper body lean into the slope.

POLES
Use your **poles** for balance, but keep them away from the skis. Do not step on the baskets.

ARMS
Hold the arms away from the body, to aid balance, and keep apart baskets and skis.

SKIS
Keep your skis parallel and across the **fall line**. Unless you maintain this position you will **slide** forward or back.

WEIGHT
You have now **transferred** the **weight** to the uphill ski, ready to bring the lower ski up parallel to it.

SKILL

DAY 1

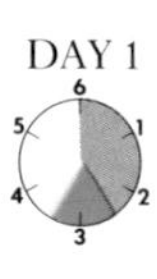

6 Changing Direction

Definition: *Shifting the direction you want to ski in, so you can start skiing*

To start skiing or move away, you usually have to turn, or change direction, in a tight space. The common error to avoid is putting one ski down across the **tail** of the other, and finding you cannot move. Make small, controlled moves – as for this **star turn**.

Star turn for gentle slopes

OBJECTIVE: To learn to turn neatly and within the space available. *Rating* ••••

On the Flat

Imagine your skis are the hands on a clock

Step 1

Initiating a Turn

Begin with your skis together, then lift the front of one ski and swing it round about 30cm (1ft), keeping the **tail** on the ground next to the other ski. Support this with a firm **pole plant**.

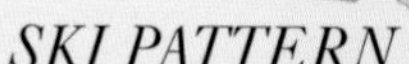

SKI PATTERN

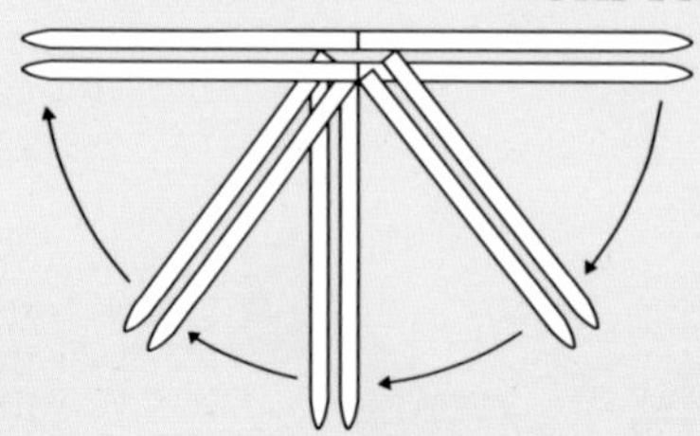

Think of the skis as hands on a clock face, pivoting from the **tail** of the ski (left). It is also possible to turn by putting the ski **tips** together, but the principles of small, controlled movements and **weight transfer** remain the same. Practise with a 180° **star turn** as shown here and observe the pattern your skis make on the snow.

BENT KNEE
The skier's weight is now completely and firmly on the right-hand ski, the knee is slightly bent to maintain balance, which is also maintained with the right-hand ski pole.

BODY
Stay in balance at all times. To do this, **transfer** your **weight** to the ski and stand firmly on it.

ERRORS TO AVOID
Apart from standing on the **tail** of the ski, the most common error in the **star turn** is to get tangled up with your poles.

Step 2
MOVING ROUND

Once you have grasped the basic principle, practise the **star turn** on flat ground. You may need to **edge** the skis to keep in balance, while you bring the second up to the first.

ARMS
Keeping the arms wide helps your balance and stops your skis coming down on your **pole** baskets.

Step 3
TURNING ROUND

In this last part of the sequence the left ski is completely **unweighted** and ready to move up to the right ski. Lift the left ski a little to clear any inequalities in the snow's surface.

WEIGHT
Unweight one ski. Move it a small way and transfer your weight to it.

HEAD
Don't look down. Turning on skis should be natural. There is no need to look down at your skis in order to see where they are. Feel for it.

SKIS
Keep the weight over the right ski, so you can unweight the left.

SKILL
6

ON THE SLOPE

*With the **star turn** grasped, practise turning the skis towards the **fall line***

Steps 1-3

MOVING AROUND

The skier is completely secure and ready to turn. The skis are across the **fall line**, while the **poles** are braced down the slope, ready to support the skier during the turn and prevent any premature start. If necessary, the skis can be **edged** into the slope as a further brake.

LOOK
Decide first where you are going and how.

WEIGHT FORWARD
Do not let the arms become straight. They will provide sufficient support if you keep them slightly bent at the elbows and not too far forward. Stay in balance at all times.

LEGS
The feet and legs are together, the weight is forward and the knees can be turned into the slope to **edge** the skis and provide insurance against a downhill slip.

STARTING DOWNHILL

OBSERVING OBSTACLES
Starting downhill does not mean simply turning your skis downhill and "bombing" to the bottom of the slope. Before you start, study the slope, decide what you are going to do and where you are going to do it. Consider the obstacles in the way; there may be a **mogul** patch or some ice to avoid; there may be other skiers coming down; there may well be a ski class standing exactly where you would like to turn. Ski classes tend to move *en masse* and may be no more in control than you.

FEAR OF FALLING
Do not be afraid of the **fall line**. As you will learn, the fall line is your friend, and provides the point around which your skiing will improve, as you tackle steeper slopes at greater speeds. When you are standing at the top of of the slope, get ready to start by changing direction as illustrated on the previous pages, and use your **ski poles** to maintain your position until you are facing in the right direction and ready to start. Don't be nervous about falling – you've learnt the best way to fall.

Step 4

READY TO GO

You have now changed the skis from facing at right angles across the **fall line,** to pointing down the fall line. If you keep the skis firmly **edged** and the **poles** braced you will not move; ease off both and you will start to ski.

A BRACING GRIP
Adopt the grip above, to help you brace yourself against the **gravity** of the slope.

SKILL

7 SNOW PLOUGH

DAY 1

Definition: *The basic and most useful method of slowing, turning, and stopping on skis*

LEARN THE **SNOW PLOUGH** and you learn how to slow down on icy paths or at the end of a run, or when going up to a ski lift, or in a dozen other situations, when a more graceful turn is not appropriate or not possible. The snow plough is the only way of slowing down without changing direction.

OBJECTIVE: To learn speed control, and stopping. *Rating* •••••

Step 1

BASIC POSITION

Feel the body relaxed with the weight over the hips and leaning slightly forward. Avoid sitting or leaning backwards. Face squarely down the **fall line**, with your weight balanced equally over both skis so that, though "V"-shaped and **edged,** they will slide evenly down the slope under control. Vary speed by pressing the knees inwards equally to ensure grip.

ARMS
Arms away from body and slightly forward of the hips. **Poles** held loosely to rear.

EDGES
The ski **edges** are your brakes. You apply or slacken them by adjusting the angle of your feet, flattening the skis or edging them to let the ski run or slow down. Try to maintain a neat ski "V" shape, or you'll **slide** off to one side or the other.

Fall line

Legs slightly "knock-kneed"

RIGHT STANCE
The **snow plough** can be tiring over any distance, and requires good technique if it is to be executed properly and with little effort. Remember to use your weight: down through the legs to the **edges** of the skis, rather than exerting pressure with excessive use of the muscles. Feel relaxed and flexible, but allow your weight to rest at the front of the boot, pressing forward with the shin to keep it there.

• **HIP CONTROL**
Keep the hips forward, over the knees and heels, so that the weight is under control and running vertically right down to the boots and skis. Avoid **flexing** the hips unduly, and maintain a basic position that is fairly upright (unless the slope is very steep). Keep the back straight and the shoulders slightly rounded, with arms away from the body and **poles** held back or wide.

Step 2

BRAKING ACTION

See the skis (below) pointing down at the **fall line**. You control the braking by widening or narrowing the "V" angle. To control the speed on a narrow path, you can increase the amount of **edge**.

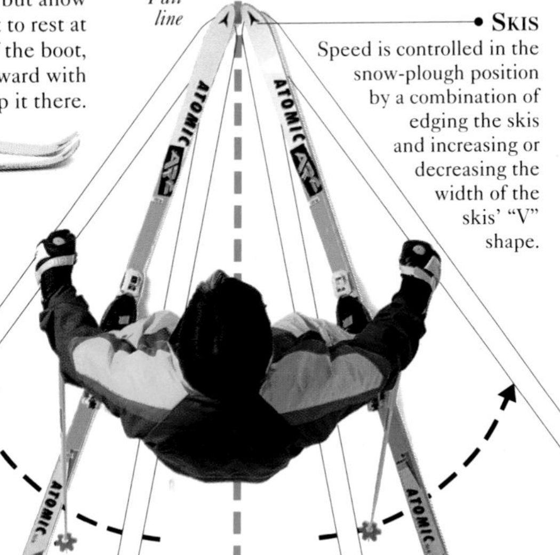

• **SKIS**
Speed is controlled in the snow-plough position by a combination of edging the skis and increasing or decreasing the width of the skis' "V" shape.

THE BRAKING SNOWPLOUGH

SHAPING UP YOUR "V"S
The **snow plough** controls speed by creating friction against the snow. The object is to achieve control without excessive and tiring effort, but it will depend on the steepness and width of the slope and state of the snow. Initiate the snow plough by spreading the skis wide while still flat and forming the "V" position (left). To do this turn the feet in and push out with the heels. Do not let the **tips** overlap. Bending the knees in causes the skis to **edge.** You can then adjust the amount of edge and the degree of width. Remember: don't let the back go hollow or sit back, sticking out the rear.

SKILL

7 THE SNOW PLOUGH STOP IN ACTION

The **snow plough** stop is simply an exaggeration of the braking needed to achieve the controlled snow plough brake. Push out your feet until you have come to a stop: this enhances the snow plough's braking effect.

HEAD
Head up, look forward. Do not look down at your skis, but note, without looking, that the **tips** are close together and in the classic "V" shape.

BODY
To feel the body balanced, keep the hips on an imaginary centre line drawn right through the "V" of the ski **tips.** Don't let the body sag backwards or fall to one side or the other.

WEIGHT
Use your weight rather than muscular effort. Feel your weight flowing onto the skis through the hips, knees and the balls of your feet.

SHOULDERS
Keep the shoulders relaxed and slightly rounded. Feel as if there is a bow or horse-shoe drawn round the shoulders from one hand to the other.

KNEES
Keep the knees pushed forward and inward to turn the skis onto their inside **edge.**

"V"-SHAPING INTO THE FALL LINE

WEIGHT & CONTROL

Weight and balance work far more for you than muscular effort, because your muscles tire quickly and this makes learning to ski difficult and exhausting. Remember that the **snow plough** consists of two main elements: the "V" shape of the skis into the fall line, and the braking effect of the edges. You can use these two elements separately or in combination, depending on the circumstances, but used together they are a simple but effective method of slowing or stopping your skis.

PRACTICE MAKES PERFECT

The **snow plough** is the most crucial skiing skill that calls for practice to perfect the technique. What it provides is control, and having control of your skis is the key to skiing without fear.

TOTAL CONTROL

By opening and closing your skis and applying and releasing the **edges,** it is possible to control the speed of descent directly down the **fall line.** Control on the steeper slopes requires much practice.

SKILL

8 SCHUSSING

DAY 1

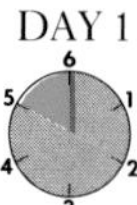

Definition: *"Straight running", or skiing straight downhill*

ALL SKIERS ENJOY a downhill run, straight down the **fall line**. This is referred to as a **schuss**, and a good schuss is one of the most enjoyable parts of skiing. It is also one of the simplest skiing skills, but it does require control and a certain amount of basic technique to maintain the correct skiing position, and to control the speed.

OBJECTIVE: To ski downhill in control, with skis parallel. *Rating* •

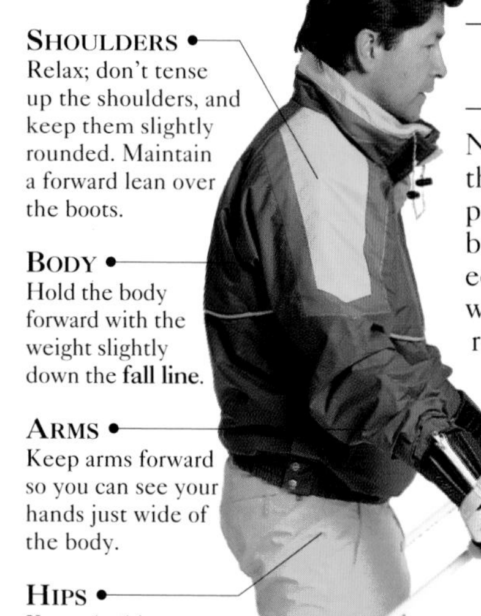

SHOULDERS • Relax; don't tense up the shoulders, and keep them slightly rounded. Maintain a forward lean over the boots.

BODY • Hold the body forward with the weight slightly down the **fall line**.

ARMS • Keep arms forward so you can see your hands just wide of the body.

HIPS • Keep the hips forward and over the knees. Avoid sitting back in the boots.

SHINS • To keep the weight forward try pressing your shins against the front of your boots. Knees should be over the toes of the boots.

FEET • Do not let your weight sag back onto your heels. Keep the weight on the balls of your feet, and therefore more on the front of your skis.

BASIC SCHUSS STANCE

Note the skier (below) is going straight down the **fall line** in a relaxed and comfortable position. His skis are parallel but slightly apart, flat and equally **weighted**, arms wide and **poles** to the rear. Adopt the **schuss** posture (left).

Fall line

RELAX
The **schuss** is an easy ski skill. Let the skis do their work of carrying you smoothly down the slope, while you lean forward; keep your balance, and let the skis run.

FAULT FINDER

DON'T TENSE UP

The big mistake in **schussing** is to be too tense. Remember to be alert to your surroundings. There will be other skiers about and you must avoid them. Always be sure that you can stop, while maintaining a relaxed, upright stance. Study these two poor skiing positions carefully because they illustrate several of the most common errors. Remember your posture checks in front of a mirror (p. 25). Also, on a sunny day you can often correct your position by studying your shadow. With practice the correct skiing position becomes instinctive.

TIPPED

This skier has the wrong forward lean. The shoulders should be back, the knees bent, and the posture relaxed.

Too tense

SLOUCHED

The weight is too far to the rear and the skier is off balance. He must bring the arms forward and get the weight over the boots.

Too laid back

VIEW FROM ABOVE

Looking down on the skier, it is easy to see how the weight is distributed evenly on both skis and down the **fall line**. This enables the skier to adjust his weight and turn in either direction.

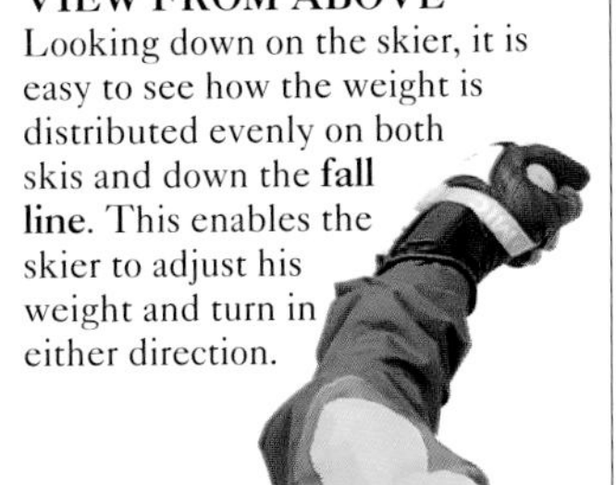

Fall line

HEAD
Keep the head up, looking forward and well ahead. You must look ahead and keep a wide vision in order to avoid other skiers.

SKIS
Leave the skis flat on the snow and keep parallel, feet apart and pointing forward. This helps prevent the ski **tips** crossing, which can cause a fall. Keep the weight forward over the front of the skis.

LEGS
Flex the legs to take up the shock of any bumps, and to act as absorbers for any pressure coming up from the skis. Keep legs slightly

POLES APART
Keep the poles wide of the body and the baskets to the rear. Do not let the baskets trail in the snow.

SKILL

9 THE SNOW-PLOUGH TURN

Definition: *To* ***weight, unweight,*** *turn the skis and change direction*

THE **SNOW-PLOUGH TURN** is the basic turn, and the basis for all other turns. It remains useful throughout your skiing career – employing many techniques that come up again and again.

OBJECTIVE: To turn neatly, to and fro, across the fall line. *Rating* ••••

Step 1

INITIATING THE TURN

Weight transfer is the key to this turn. Transfer the weight to one leg and swing in the opposite direction. Weight on the right leg swings you to the left, and vice-versa.

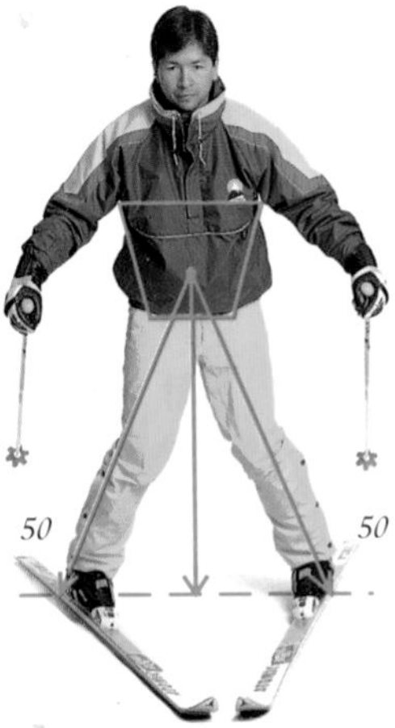

50 *50*

WEIGHT DISTRIBUTION
To stay in the **snow plough** keep your weight evenly distributed. To **initiate** a turn, **transfer** 90 per cent of your **weight** onto one ski as shown.

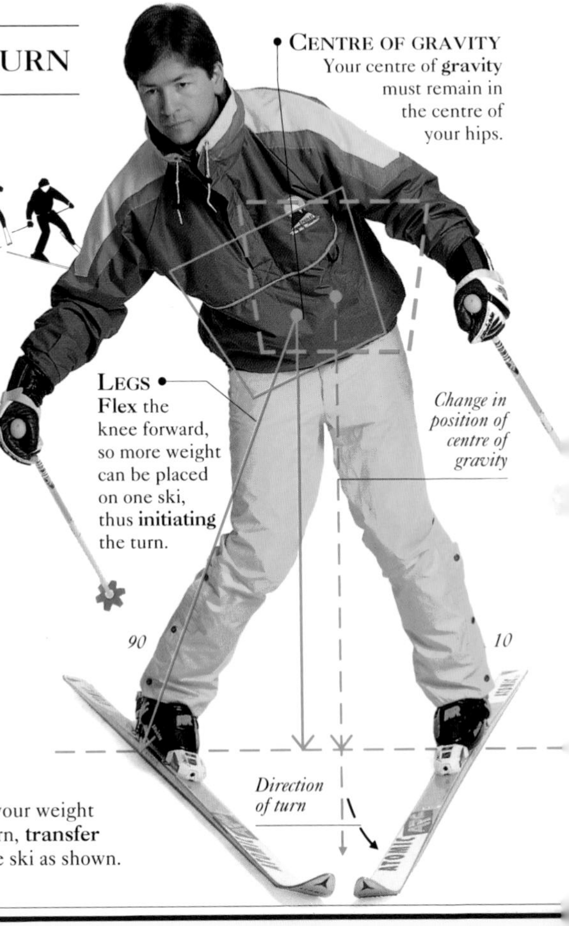

CENTRE OF GRAVITY
Your centre of **gravity** must remain in the centre of your hips.

LEGS
Flex the knee forward, so more weight can be placed on one ski, thus **initiating** the turn.

Change in position of centre of gravity

90 *10*

Direction of turn

HEAD
Look in the direction in which you are travelling. Do not look down at your skis.

UPPER BODY
Hold your balance, keeping your weight on the right-hand ski, which swings you to the left. Do not let your body fall back, but keep the upper body forward and the weight on the turning ski.

ARMS
Keep the arms wide and away from the body, and imagine that you are turning a giant wheel as the skis turn across the **fall line**. This keeps in balance when you immediately go into a new turn.

POLES
The **poles** have very little to do at this time. Keep them clear of the snow, using them only for balance.

Step 2

WEIGHT TRANSFER

Keep the skis ploughed, but reduce the degreee of **edge.** Increase the speed of **weight transfer** from one ski to the other, and do this close to the **fall line**. Do not allow the skis to turn fullly parallel to the slope.

MAKING YOUR KNEES DO THE WORK

PUSHING WITH THE KNEES

The knees have a big part to play in skiing, particularly in controlling the amount of **edge** you put on the skis, and in steering the skis round the turn. In the **snow-plough turn** you should feel your knees working on the edges, and push your knees in the direction you wish to travel. As with many skiing movements, this is something you must learn until it becomes second nature, and you move into the right position naturally. Study the illustrations on these pages to see how the knees govern the position of the ski **edges,** and body posture, in the snow-plough turn. Practise pushing the knees.

SKI EDGES

The ski edges are your brakes. Edge one ski more than another by turning the knee in and you will force that ski to turn. The knees control the edges: the skier (right) has turned in his left knee slightly below the right knee, putting more edge on the left ski than on the right ski. Practise changing edges like this, exaggerating the movement in order to feel the effects.

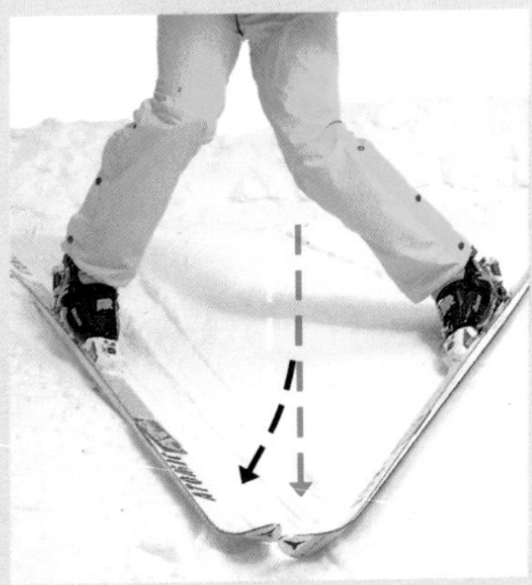

SKILL
9

Step 3

COMPLETING A TURN

LEGS
Keep the turning leg bent, **steering** that ski with the knee.

To stop at the end of a turn, simply keep the pressure on the turning ski and it will turn across the slope. You can then come to a stop, bring your skis together, and prepare to start again. To practise linked turns, turn when the skis are across the **fall line**, straightening the knee and moving the weight across the other ski, thus **initiating** a turn in the other direction.

WEIGHTING
Put 80 per cent of your weight on the turning ski. Use weight, not muscles, to put pressure on the ski.

SKIS
Maintain the **snow plough** throughout, to provide some braking action. More can be supplied by **edging** the skis.

RELAXING INTO THE SNOW-PLOUGH TURN

The **snow-plough turn** may look simple, but it is as prone to error as any other skiing skill. Don't let your body become tense. Avoid tiring yourself out by using your muscles to wrench the skis round. Don't let your skis go too wide or you may find yourself doing the splits. Above all, don't rush it. Give the snow-plough turn a chance to work.

UPRIGHT
Stay upright. Don't sit back, or bend the upper body forward.

WRONG TURN
Don't attempt to turn by swinging the shoulders round. This will put you off-balance.

PRACTICE
Getting it right may take a little practice, but if you work gently, and turn smoothly across the fall line, you will find it fun and quite easy.

TURNING RIGHT OR LEFT

Practise linked **snow-plough turns** to the left and right. Note from the skier (below) that he **initiates** turns by moving his weight, pushing on one ski to turn in the other direction, but the ski **tips** remain pointing down the slope, swinging to and fro across the **fall line**. Aim for a flowing rhythm.

SMOOTH SWINGS

Don't rush these turns. Have patience. Put the pressure on and then give the ski time to work. The object is to achieve smooth, even swings to and fro across the **fall line**, and to achieve this you must move smoothly but firmly to **initiate** the turn, and keep the pressure on until the turn is completed.

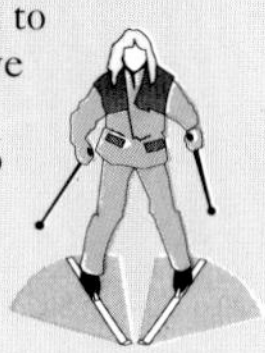

SHOULDERS Keep the shoulders calm and avoid wild swings of the upper body. It may help if you drop your turning shoulder slightly to put more weight and pressure on the turning ski.

ARMS Keep your arms wide. If you imagine that you are holding a large steering wheel, this will help you maintain the right position. Keep the hands forward at waist height.

BODY Head and body face down the slope and move only enough for **weight transfer** from one ski to the other. Avoid swinging the shoulders about.

LEGS Use your legs to put pressure on the turning ski, bending the knee forward to steer the ski round.

SHINS Press with the shins against the front of your boot, and keep the feet turned in so the ski tips stay together.

Fall line

SKILL

9

SHOULDERS
Keep the shoulder over the turning ski to gain the correct body position, and to shift your weight.

HEAD
Looking down the slope, get your head over the turning ski.

POLES
You do not need the **poles** for the **snow-plough turn.** Keep them off the snow and away from your body.

KNEES
Roll the knee lower in, to keep the correct **edge** and the **snow-plough** position.

WEIGHT TRANSFER
Begin **weight transfer** to the right-hand ski, bending the knee. The weight automatically comes over the ski to **initiate** the turning movement. Use weight rather than muscle power.

HOLDING THE PLOUGH SHAPE

Work the boots and skis together to maintain the "V" shape of the **snow plough**. Don't alter this position, because you achieve the **snow-plough turn** simply by **weight transfer,** and by applying a degree of pressure to the turning ski. Observe how to make a turn across the **fall line** by transferring the weight onto one ski. Weight, **unweight,** and **edge** the ski, while keeping both skis in the snow plough. The result is a series of even turns down the slope, across the fall line.

LEGS
Flex the legs at the knee, but press the shin firmly against the front of the boot.

TIPS FOR SNOW-PLOUGH TURNING

MIRROR IMAGE
Although this is a simple turn, it takes practice and technique. Study the sequence below carefully, and then copy it in front of a mirror. Don't let the ski **tips** cross.

Overworking the turning ski leads quickly to being tired. Lean out of the turn; do not lean forward or back. In your efforts to turn, do not let the lower shoulder turn across the slope or your weight will rotate onto the wrong ski. Be sure to maintain the correct **snow-plough** position at the start of the turn, using your weight and pressure in the turn, until you are ready to turn again, across the **fall line,** in the other direction.

WEIGHING IN
Aim to turn using your knees and the feet, not by swinging your shoulders. Do not jerk your body. Use your weight rather than physical effort.

AWARENESS
Be sure you are not turning across the path of another skier. Keep looking down the slope. Do not turn your head uphill.

COMPLETING THE TURN
Take the pressure off the lower ski slightly as you cross the **fall line,** bringing your shoulders and hips back to put the weight evenly between the skis once more.

Arms bent slightly at elbows, in front of body

WEIGHT
Now put the weight on the other ski and turn to the right.

SKILL

10 Traversing

DAY 2

Definition: *Skiing across the slope while maintaining your height on the mountain*

Traversing is an essential but enjoyable skiing skill that helps you check your speed and control down the ski run, and your direction relative to the **fall line**. Using turns at the end of each **traverse**, it is possible to descend the slope at whatever speed you desire – the steeper the traverse the greater the speed. You maintain your desired height across the slope by **edging** firmly into it, preventing the skis **slipping** sideways, and you from falling onto the uphill slope.

OBJECTIVE: To ski across any slope, however steep, in a secure and confident manner. *Rating* •••

Weight Have 90 per cent of your weight on the lower ski. Keep the weight forward. Do not sit back.

Hips Distribute your weight by turning the hips into the slope.

Knees **Flex** knees well forward and turn them into the slope to increase the amount of **edging** needed for your desired speed and position.

Comma Position

The basic **traverse** stance of the skier (left), is also called the **comma** because of the shape. The skier looks ahead, leaning out slightly, with the knees and feet **edged** into the slope across the **fall line**, the upper body slightly in front so the skier faces down and across the fall line with a good view.

Skis Upper edged ski slightly in front of lower edged ski.

PULLED INTO POSITION

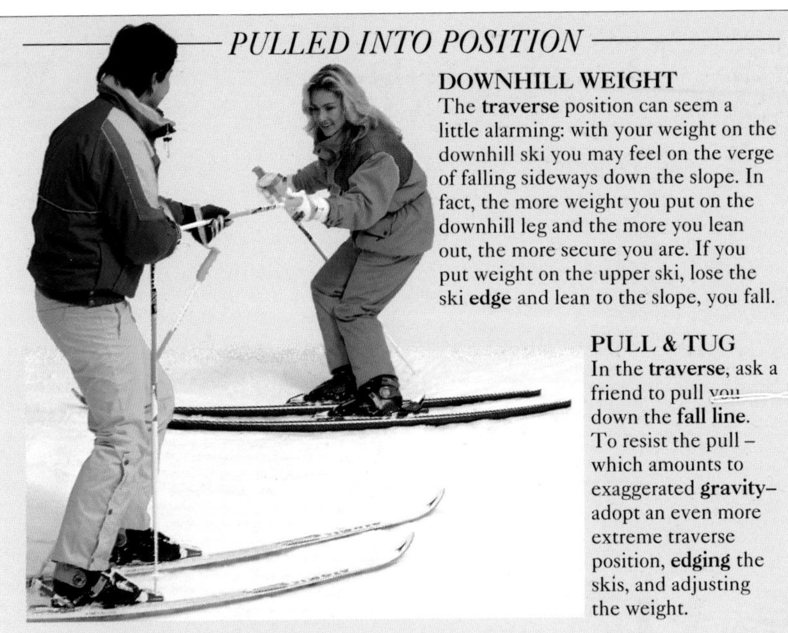

DOWNHILL WEIGHT

The **traverse** position can seem a little alarming: with your weight on the downhill ski you may feel on the verge of falling sideways down the slope. In fact, the more weight you put on the downhill leg and the more you lean out, the more secure you are. If you put weight on the upper ski, lose the ski **edge** and lean to the slope, you fall.

PULL & TUG

In the **traverse**, ask a friend to pull you down the **fall line**. To resist the pull – which amounts to exaggerated **gravity**– adopt an even more extreme traverse position, **edging** the skis, and adjusting the weight.

BIRD'S EYE VIEW

Study the position carefully, viewed here from above, and notice how the skis are parallel across the **fall line**, with the upper ski half a boot's length in front. The weight is over the lower ski, and the skier looks ahead and slightly downhill. Seen from above, the skier's balance is easy to judge.

UPHILL SKI •
About 10 per cent of the body weight rests on the uphill ski in the **traverse,** just enough to maintain balance; but be ready to transfer all your weight to it as you enter the turn.

ARMS •
For balance, keep the arms wide, slightly bent, and forward of the body at all times. Keep the pole baskets clear of the snow.

UPPER BODY •
Turn the torso so that the upper shoulder is slightly in the lead. This keeps the weight forward and allows you to look down the **fall line**, with weight on downhill ski.

SKIS •
Push into the slope to secure the skis with the uphill **edges** – the amount of edge depending on the degree of steepness, with the upper ski slightly in front.

SKILL

11 Timing

DAY 2

Definition: *Using poles for pivoting in a turn*

Use **ski poles** to help you pivot in a turn and to assist in **unweighting** during a turn, as well as for balance. Ski poles are invaluable in the timing of a turn. Once you have learnt the **snow plough**, try using your ski poles to improve unweighting.

OBJECTIVE: To time your **pole planting** correctly. *Rating*• • •

Step 1

Pole Plant

Use the **pole** in the **traverse** to provide assistance in the **weight transfer** to the outer ski, to help in maintaining balance, and for the **unweighting** process, which ensures a smooth turn. Hold the pole firmly, and **plant** it at a comfortable distance forward, without over-reaching.

FROM THE TRAVERSE
The skier (right) is **initiating** a turn from the **snow plough** with the downhill ski, and putting weight upon it.

Knees
Planting the **pole** triggers you to bend your knees to begin the first part of the **unweighting** action. Unless your body goes down, it cannot come up. As the body goes down, it brings the ski pole naturally towards the snow.

Arms
Pole plant with the arm slightly bent. Don't straighten the arm or strain forward, or your balance is bound to suffer.

Body
The body maintains the correct position, but is starting to go down as the **pole** is **planted.**

Skis
Keep the lower ski **edged** and **weighted.**

TURNING
Run past the **pole** in the snow, halfway between boot and ski **tip**, with your weight coming up and forward as you turn.

Step 2

UNWEIGHTING

Unweighting means reducing the amount of pressure on the skis by an upward extension of your body. This enables you to make a smooth turn. You unweight the skis by stretching, or **extending**, the body just before the turn, as you go past the **ski pole.**

LEGS AND KNEES
The legs and knees drive the skis along and into the turn. Keep the knees bent and the shin pressed against the front of the boot, releasing pressure on the boot as you pass the **ski pole.**

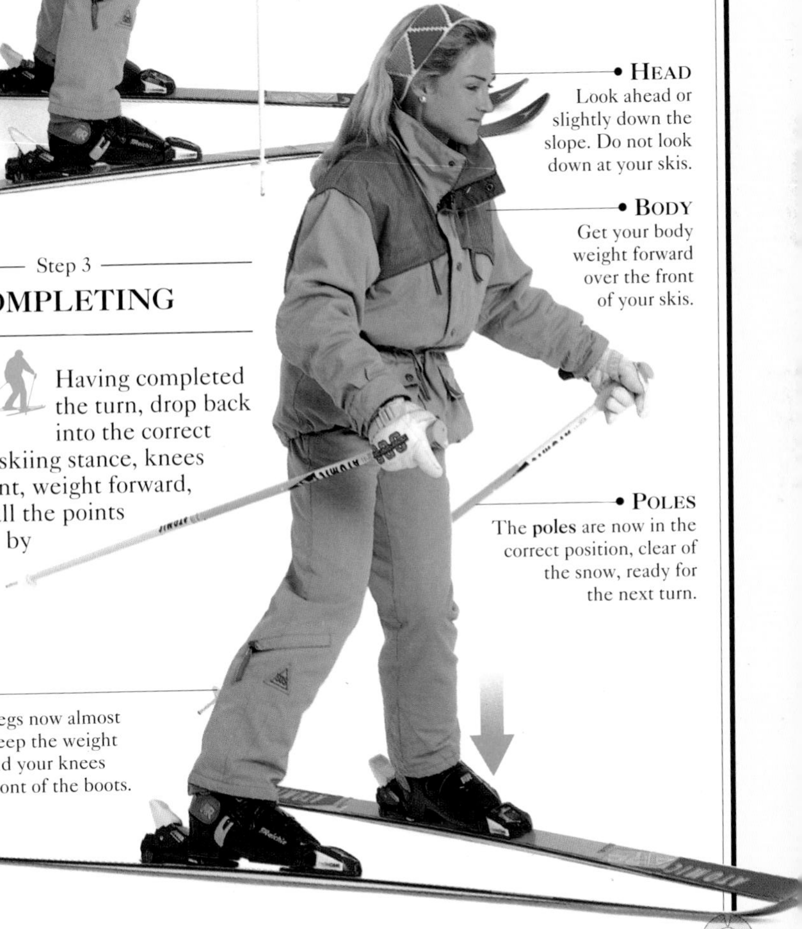

HEAD
Look ahead or slightly down the slope. Do not look down at your skis.

BODY
Get your body weight forward over the front of your skis.

Step 3

COMPLETING

Having completed the turn, drop back into the correct skiing stance, knees bent, weight forward, head up... all the points that should, by now, be becoming instinctive.

POLES
The **poles** are now in the correct position, clear of the snow, ready for the next turn.

LEGS
With the legs now almost straight, keep the weight forward and your knees over the front of the boots.

SKILL

11 POLE PLANT IN ACTION

If you time your **pole planting** correctly and put the pole down in the correct place, you will go a long way to achieving a smooth turn and the correct **weight transfer** onto the turning ski. The sequence here illustrates the correct time and place for pole planting during a turn to the right.

UPPER BODY
Do not swing the upper body. Keep it calm.

UNUSED POLE
Keep the unused pole out of the way, and the arm still. Do not bring your arm across in front of your body.

KNEES
Steer the ski round the turn using the outer knee. Keep it pushed forward so the shin presses firmly into the front of the boot.

LEGS
As you pass the **pole,** stand up to **unweight** the skis. This upward movement sweeps you round the pole, after which you will sink down again. Keep this upward and downward movment smooth.

AS YOUR CONFIDENCE GROWS

OVER VIEW

See how the skier prepares to plant the pole while keeping shoulders parallel.

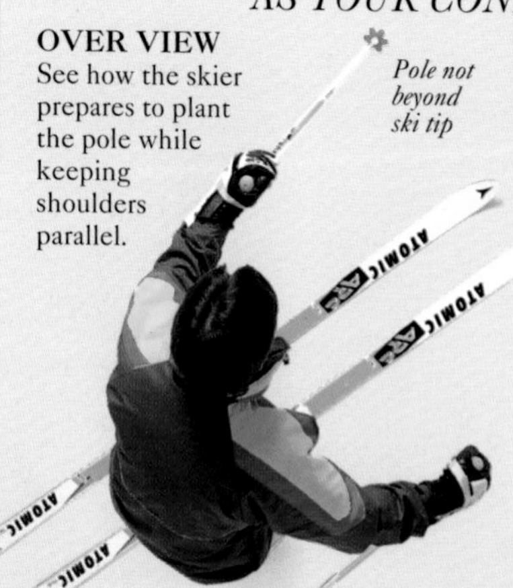

Pole not beyond ski tip

DEVELOPING RHYTHM

Like all ski movements, your **pole planting** will be more successful if you make the movements smoothly but firmly, swinging your body round the planted pole and back into the required position. As you work closer and closer to the fall line you will find it necessary to plant the pole more quickly as you make shorter turns. Look around the ski slope and you find skiers doing just that, making short turns, straight down the **fall line,** planting their poles left and right in rapid succession. The effect of this is to control your speed, so find a slope of about 30 °, and practise coming down as straight as possible, making continuous turns, one after the other, as quickly as possible in rhythm.

BODY
After turning, much of your weight will be on the downhill ski, which allows the upper ski to slide in. You can adopt the **traverse** and prepare to turn again. At this point both poles are clear of the snow.

HEAD
Look ahead and decide exactly where you are going to turn, and think about the sequence. Above all, do not look down at your skis.

EYES
Look ahead to pick and time your next turning point.

HIPS
Keep the hips pointed in the direction of travel, even when, as here, the lower knee is bent with the lower ski absorbing much of the weight. Note also that the lower ski is **edged.**

PREPARING
When preparing to turn, drop half down and forward, ready for the **unweighting** that must follow as the body comes up again. Do not reach forward with the arm when **planting** the **pole** – this causes the lower shoulder to swing forward and puts your body out of balance.

WEIGHT
As you **plant** your **pole,** ensure that 80 per cent of your weight is transferred to your lower ski.

POLE PLANT
Plant the **pole** near the ski **tip,** with a firm downward movement, the pole slanted slightly forward. Keep the pole away from the ski or you may run over the basket.

SKILL

DAY 2

12 SIDE-SLIPPING

Definition: *A safe sliding movement sideways down the slope, on the* ***fall line***

The beginner may find **slide-slipping** a little difficult because it relies very much on the correct use of **weight transfer** and **edging,** and requires you to lean out down the slope. On the other hand, it is a most enjoyable manoeuvre and very useful.

OBJECTIVE: To lose height without losing direction. *Rating* ••••

Step 1

SLIPPING

From the **traverse,** with your weight on the downhill ski, lean out – with your knees away from the slope – and flatten the downhill ski to lose the **edge** that grips the snow. Your flattened skis then start to slide down.

SKI TIPS

ON AND OFF THE EDGE
One of the great advantages of learning **side-slipping,** apart from mastering a safe way to decend down a slope, is that it gives you a great sense of what is happening to your skis, as you turn them onto and off their **edges.** You can turn your skis in various directions by rolling from one edge to the other, and practise improves both your ski control and confidence.

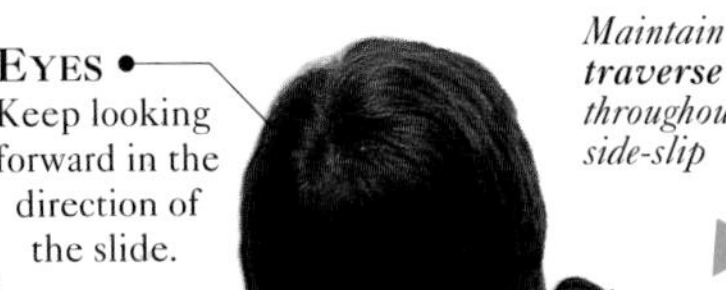

EYES Keep looking forward in the direction of the slide.

Maintain ***traverse*** *throughout side-slip*

Fall line

OVERVIEW
You are in the **traverse,** running across the **fall line.** Now put your weight over the downhill ski, roll the ski flat to lose the **edge,** and move your weight slightly forward. The skis will now start to slip naturally sideways down the slope.

• BODY
As you stop, get your body facing down the **fall line**, not in the direction of your skis. In this position, leaning out slightly down the slope, you will be very secure, and resting on your ski **edges**.

Step 3

STOPPING

To stop the **side-slip**, simply **edge** the skis, and as the edges bite, the slide will stop and the forward **traverse** commence once again.

Fall line

• SKIS
The skis are now **edged** and the **tips** are turned slightly uphill from the **fall line.**

TIPS UP
To stop **sliding** diagonally across the slope, turn the **tips** of the skis uphill, and increase the amount of **edge.** Now across the direction of travel, you will stop.

LEARNING EDGE CONTROL

FEEL WITH YOUR FEET
In the **side-slip** you can travel sideways and down, but also forward. To avoid falling over you must be positive and keep your weight away from the slope. Do not lean in. Notice that the ankles are turned out and the knees are straight. Put more weight on the downhill ski.

1 Apply your weight to the downhill ski and lean away from the slope. Turn the ankles out, flattening the **edges.**

2 To regain the **traverse, edge** the skis into the slope and turn the knees into the slope keeping your weight forward.

SKILL

12

CONTROL

Initiate the **side-slip** with skis parallel. Lean your weight out, away from the slope, and let the skis **slide** sideways down the slope, but under control. By rocking on the **edges** you can control your speed and keep the slide even.

SKIS
With skis parallel and slightly apart, roll the ankles to flatten the ski.

KNEES
Keep the knees together, and bend them forward and out, rocking them to and fro to release or regain the **edges.**

LEARNING TO LEAN OUT

ROLL AND TURN THE KNEES

The steeper the slope the more you must lean out, rolling the knees out to start the slide (left). Turn the knees into the slope getting the uphill edges to bite into the snow to regain the traverse position (right). Keep the body turned down the slope and the weight over the downhill ski. Then flatten the skis and your weight will produce the slide. You may need to press down on the heels to get the **slide-slip** going. Practise this also on a slightly steeper slope and on hard snow.

Unweighting

Weighting

SIDE-SLIPPING IN SEQUENCE

Observe this **side-slipping** sequence down the **fall line,** and the process of coming to a stop. The lower you get, the quicker you stop. Notice that the position of the skier hardly varies. The weight is down, and you must push down with your legs while rolling the knees out to flatten the skis and start the **slide**. Do not let the knees become straight. It takes constant practice, but you will find that you can slide down a slope under complete control.

SKILL

13 READING THE SLOPE

DAY 2

Definition: *To anticipate, and so avoid, accidents*

LEARNING THE BASIC SKI SKILLS, either at home or on the slopes, is the essence of this course. But, in addition to these skills, you must also take into consideration varied terrain, and unpredictable skiers.

OBJECTIVE: To be aware of ever-changing conditions. *Rating* ••••

OBSTACLES

Learn to recognize the hidden dangers on the slope

• CHILDREN
Watch out for youngsters coming down the slope with confidence but no skill.

• FALLEN SKIERS
Avoid any fallen skier on the piste.

• SKI SCHOOL
Be aware that in a few minutes – after the ski instructor has warmed up his class and got their muscles flexible – this ski school will be taking up a great deal of the available slope space.

GETTING AN OVERVIEW

Here is a typical view you can expect as you are about to make your run. Take a look at how many obstacles – man-made and natural – you can identify, and think about how you would tackle them.

—LEARNING TO SKI SAFELY AND EFFICIENTLY—

BENEFITS OR HAZARDS?

Reading a ski slope is not as simple as it might appear (see also pp.90-91). There are all types of potential hazards that you must assess, but with practice you will take all this in very quickly, come to a decision, and act upon it. You cannot expect to find empty **pistes** very often, and if a piste run is completely empty perhaps there is a good reason for it. Maybe you have missed the avalanche warning. In any event, remember that ski slopes offer you potential benefits and potential hazards. Learn to recognize the one and avoid the other before you can call yourself a competent skier. Ski resort aids turn into "hazards" only because you are not concentrating. For example, if you listen out in thick mist, the noise of a ski lift can help direct your way down.

ADAPT TO THE UNEXPECTED

Many factors determine how you adapt your skills for a particular ski run – other skiers near you, constantly changing weather, visibility, and terrain for instance – so read the slope carefully and judge your speed accordingly.

SKI LIFT PYLONS
The snow will be deep and ungroomed near pylons, and there may be hidden holes. Stay away from ski pylons and never ski down between them. Use a ski lift as a point of reference on the slope.

PISTE MACHINE
Watch out for surprisingly fast **piste bashers,** as they can change direction without warning.

ROCKS
Watch out for exposed rocks at the sides of a **piste.**

MOGULS
These **moguls** are not very large, but they could be a problem. (See pages 74-75.)

DEEP SHADOW
If you ski out of the sunlight into shadow, your vision will be affected for a few seconds. In shadow you will find hard snow, frozen crust, or ice.

SKILL

13

BUMPS AND DIPS

Coping with varying surfaces

FLEX AND EXTEND

Don't worry about bumps and dips: if you keep the body relaxed and the knees bent, you can ride out a sudden change in the surface by **flexing** and **extending** the knees and body. Apart from flexing the knees, keep looking ahead, stay in balance, and keep your weight forward.

HEAD • Keep looking ahead and study the terrain. When approaching a dip or bump, get ready for it by adusting your weight to control speed.

• **ARMS** Keep the arms wide to act as aids to maintaining balance.

• **UPPER BODY** Bumps or dips can throw you forward or back on your heels. Counteract this by keeping the body relaxed but not loose, ready to act against any force that works upon it vertically, up or down.

FLEX • The knees and legs act as shock absorbers. Straighten them out in a dip, and allow them to **flex** to swallow the effect of a bump. In either case keep your upper body at an even height.

SKIS • On uneven ground, it is all too easy for your skis to cross, causing a fall. Keep the skis parallel but about 15 cm (6 in) apart, and be sure to keep them pointing forward.

FLEXING IS THE WAY TO GO

The phrase you must keep in mind is **flexing.** Keep the body relaxed, but keep the knees flexing all the time, rather like the suspension on a car. Imagine yourself going up and down, evenly, under control, riding out the variations in the terrain.

BALANCE
Balance is vital. Adust your weight at all times to stay in balance, whatever the terrain.

SCHUSSING
Keep weight forward, skis parallel, knees bent and **flexing,** ready to absorb the terrain as you approach the bump. At the dip, straighten the knees.

LOWER BODY
Extend your posture by straightening your knees and legs smoothly. Do this without throwing yourself into the air or raising the arms.

BODY
Lean the body forward down the slope. Don't let your weight fall back onto your heels.

POLES
Keep the **poles** out of the way and use them only to maintain your

EXTENSION
Extending simply means to come up on the skis, thus countering – not overcoming – any excessive movement and the effects of **gravity** as you enter a dip.

COPING WITH DEEP DEPRESSIONS

RIDING OUT THE ROUGH
Study the skier as he enters a dip in the correct position, then **extends** the body and legs to absorb the dip, going then into the **flex** posture on the rise, and then fully **flexing** or bending the knees to absorb the bump on the far side. **Flexing** and **extending** helps you to "smooth out" the bumps and dips.

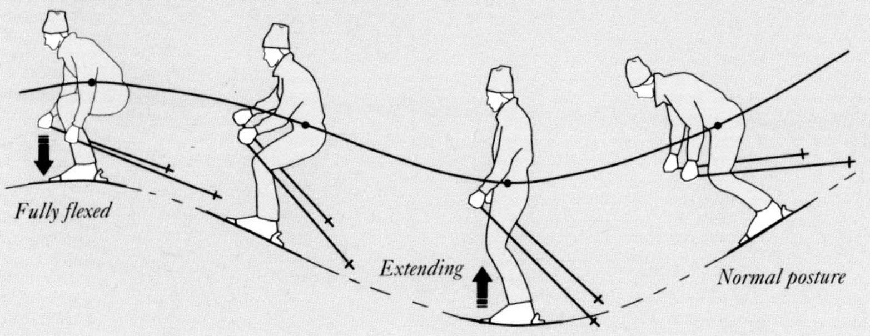

SKILL

13

Negotiating Moguls

Practising your turning technique

Turning Them to Your Advantage

Many skiers are afraid of **moguls**: but these mounds are inevitable on a ski slope, because moguls are created by the action of skis turning on the snow. You can go over moguls or round them, but once in a mogul field you can't avoid them.

INITIATE YOUR TURN

Look ahead and plot a path through the **moguls**. Start the turn in the normal way by stemming out on one ski and adjusting your weight as usual. It is necessary to control your speed and direction, and steer the ski around or over the bump.

Arms •
Hold your arms out fairly wide, and use them to maintain a balanced posture.

SKIS

Think of yourself as a rally car negotiating bumpy tracks, with the suspension keeping both wheels on the uneven surface. Likewise keep as much of the ski as possible on the snow.

• Legs
Most weight is on the downhill ski, and the legs are **steering** the skis around the **mogul.**

Upper Body •
Keep the upper body stable as you go over the **mogul**. Do not lean back or go too fast.

EXTRA WEIGHTING
Keep the weight forward to keep the **forebody** of the ski on the snow. This is the part that does the turning, and should not be allowed to rise up into the air.

MAKING CONTACT
Keep the upper body weight forward to maintain balance, and the **forebody** of the skis as far as possible in contact with the snow. Feel the pressure on the skis now pushing up through your legs – think of the rally car suspension over a bumpy track – and you'll find it necessary to **flex** the knees to ride out the bump.

LEGS
Bend the knees and **flex** the legs to absorb the upward pressure from the snow.

HEAD
Keep the head up and look ahead to anticipate more bumps.

SMOOTHING OUT THE WORRIES

THINGS THAT GO BUMP
Moguls require a certain technique. Don't be afraid of them, they are only bumps in the snow. A little speed is useful but don't go too fast. Do not lean into the bump, and do not look down at the mogul – both faults evident in this skier's posture (right). Be sure to keep the **forebody** of the ski on the snow. If you are on top of the mogul, lean out down the far side. This may seem unnatural but it keeps the **forebody** of the ski on the snow – and you will feel safe.

Incorrect stance

TURN EARLY
Turn often and turn early on moguls. Do not go bouncing on across the bumps until you run out of slope. Try to maintain a downhill line, close to the **fall line**. If you go round the side of the mogul, use your **edges** to avoid slipping into the trough. If you go over the top of the mogul, remember to turn on the top and not when **sliding** down into the far trough. Turning your skis on top can be easier than you think, because only a small area is in contact with the snow, and so there is less surface resistence.

SKILL

14 FINE TUNING

DAY 2

Definition: *Sharpening the skills already learnt*

TO IMPROVE ON WHAT you've learnt so far, set yourself small, attainable objectives, aiming to improve and refine your techniques. Here we are trying not simply to come to a **snow-plough stop,** but to slow down and stop exactly where we want to, **tips** level to the hat.

OBJECTIVE: To improve your control and refine your techniques. *Rating* •••

PRACTICE MAKES PERFECT

Using aids and objectives to improve your ski techniques

PRACTISE STOPPING

Being able to stop is a vital skiing skill. Being unable to stop is the great fear of skiers. Improving means stopping under control.

EDGES • To begin with, the **snow-plough** position will act as a brake. Increase the braking action by **edging** the skis as you slow down.

• **SKIS** Ski towards the marker in a **schuss,** then go into the **snow-plough** position with skis **edged,** gradually pressing out to reduce speed.

• **POLES** Hold the **poles** away from the skis and the body.

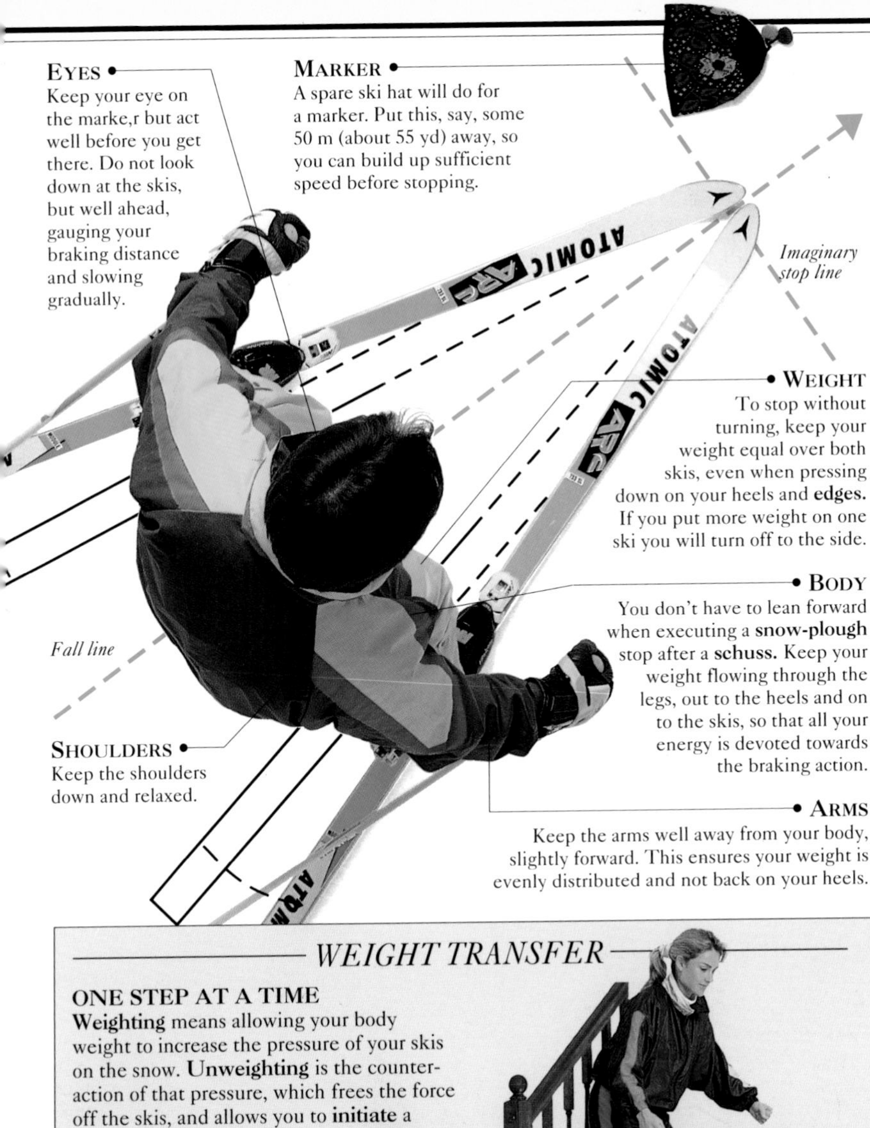

EYES
Keep your eye on the marke,r but act well before you get there. Do not look down at the skis, but well ahead, gauging your braking distance and slowing gradually.

MARKER
A spare ski hat will do for a marker. Put this, say, some 50 m (about 55 yd) away, so you can build up sufficient speed before stopping.

Imaginary stop line

WEIGHT
To stop without turning, keep your weight equal over both skis, even when pressing down on your heels and **edges.** If you put more weight on one ski you will turn off to the side.

BODY
You don't have to lean forward when executing a **snow-plough** stop after a **schuss.** Keep your weight flowing through the legs, out to the heels and on to the skis, so that all your energy is devoted towards the braking action.

Fall line

SHOULDERS
Keep the shoulders down and relaxed.

ARMS
Keep the arms well away from your body, slightly forward. This ensures your weight is evenly distributed and not back on your heels.

WEIGHT TRANSFER

ONE STEP AT A TIME

Weighting means allowing your body weight to increase the pressure of your skis on the snow. **Unweighting** is the counter-action of that pressure, which frees the force off the skis, and allows you to **initiate** a change of direction. Both are needed if you want to develop a sound skiing technique. There are a number of ways to practise this. Try it first as an exercise on the stairs at home. The objective is to concentrate on **weight transfer** from one leg to the other. Climb up the stairs sideways, as shown here, and walk straight down, as if skiing. Doing it in ski boots will feel odd and be difficult at first, but persevere, trying to maintain the correct ski position. This exercise also requires you to work on your balance.

SKILL

14 FINDING A NATURAL FEEL

Study the skier trying the **snow plough** viewed from in front. Notice how he starts in an open position (exaggerated to show the reaction) adopting a close posture as he slows down, squeezing the speed from his descent.

EYES • Concentrate on stopping in the required position, looking ahead.

STARTING POSITION

Hold an upright posture, arms out, skis across the **fall line** and not too much **edge.** Let the skis run before you apply the **edges** (brakes), with your knees.

STAND UP • Begin with body straight, back hollow, looking ahead rather than down.

HEAD • Try to stop without looking down at the skis.

Lift

LEGS • Keep the legs fairly straight to avoid excess **edging.**

ARMS • Keep the arms away from the body to aid balancing.

KNEES • The knees are still apart, though closer together than they were at the start.

–STARTING TO BRAKE–

CHANGING POSTURE

Notice how the skier (right) starts to control his speed, dropping the body down by bending the knees, bringing the arms in, and rounding the shoulders. He is literally squeezing the speed out of his descent. The weight is evenly distributed on both skis, as he slows his descent right down the **fall line.** His arms and **poles** are kept well clear from his body as an aid to balance.

SKIS • **Edge** the skis, but stay running straight down the **fall line** in the **snow plough.**

PERCHING PRACTICE

VISUALIZATION

To help improve your **traverse** technique, visualize a fence or a gate running across the **fall line**. Then see yourself placing the skis parallel to the fence, across some imaginary or actual fall line, and imagine perching alongside the fence or gate. This will automatically provide you with the right traverse position, with the hips and shoulders correctly aligned, if you turn the upper body as shown. When you are traversing, just try to visualize yourself perched on a rail. Aim to use this mental image to help you at the end of each turn, and to give you confidence in the traverse as you start your next turn. Remember to use **angulation** in the upper body, and to lean out over your downhill ski, assuming the **comma** posture. With your skis **edged**, you won't **slide** down the slope.

STANCE • Upper body leaning out, lower body pushing into the slope.

THIGHS • Press the thighs and knees tightly together and push forward. **Edge** the skis completely.

CROUCH DOWN

Observe how the skier goes from an open stance to a closed, lower posture. The faster you go from one positon to another, the faster you come to a stop.

• **BODY & BALANCE** Lean the body, arms and elbows in to resist the braking effect of the skis and to maintain balance – which remains directly in the centre of the **snow plough.** Do not allow your balance, and therefore your weight, to fall off one side or the other.

• **KNEE PRESS** By pressing the knees in with the hands, you keep the poles away from the skis and off the snow.

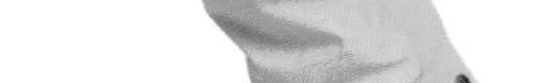

• **EDGING** Tilting the ski **edges** into the slope by bending the knees and **weighting** the body, gives you extra grip, or bite, allowing you to control your skis.

FIST PRESS

At this point it is a useful exercise to press the knees together with the fists, as this also ensures the correct body position.

AFTER THE WEEKEND

Taking your new-found skills to the slope

YOU HAVE COMPLETED the weekend ski course and you now have a firm grasp of all the basic essentials of skiing. You know how to **traverse,** how to turn, how to stop, how to fall down and how to get up again, how to run down a slope and how to get ready mentally for the demands of skiing. These are the fundamentals, and without a firm grasp of them you will never develop a sound ski technique.

ENJOY IT
Above all, make learning enjoyable. If you meet a problem, don't worry about it. Just go back to the basics, and you will soon start making progress again.

The best place to go is into a ski school, one where instructors speak your language, use terms that you can understand, and know how to analyze and solve your problems. Choose a small class if possible. Having mastered the weekend course you will be better than many of your class-mates and may feel ready for a more advanced class, or for a few private lessons to improve some of the finer points of your technique. The important thing is to keep on skiing, because nothing will improve your skiing so much as time spent on snow. The basic techniques you have grasped in the weekend course will hold good when learning to ski on more challenging terrain: higher mountains, and deeper snow, both on- and **off-piste.**

SKIS TOGETHER

The art of making smooth, linked, ***parallel turns***

EVERY BEGINNER WANTS to progress to **parallel turns**. It looks graceful, feels wonderful, but takes practice. First remember that the skis do not have to be glued together for a neat parallel turn. Keep the skis a hip's-width apart for the most stable position. Secondly, remember that both skis change their **edges** at the same time. This requires the application of all the skills you have learned, which, with a little speed and confidence, will bring your skis closer.

SPEED AND ATTACK
It is easier to bring the skis together if you ski at speed and close to the **fall line**. This skier is doing just that.

HOW SPEED HELPS

WEIGHT TRANSFER
To ski with your skis together, you must ski faster. Subsequently you will **weight** or **unweight** your skis quicker. As you transfer the weight from one ski to the other, the skis begin to turn more efficiently. Don't try to bring your skis together at once. Try to maintain an open, balanced stance: this makes speed less of a problem. Use speed into the turn, keep looking down the slope, and **initiate** the turn more quickly. There is no need to force the skis round if you are moving with speed. Speed also helps with the unweighting of the skis at the start of the turn. With speed, a relatively small upward movement of the body releases the pull of **gravity** and unweights the ski.

PRACTISE TURNING

Study this skier bringing his skis ever closer together. The skier maintains his balance over the **weighted** ski, while he brings the **unweighted** ski into the centre. Skiing at speed into the turn enables you not only to keep your skis ever more closer together, but also to **initiate** the turn by **unweighting** both skis, rather than one. This takes practice, so concentrate on turning smoothly, skiing faster, and bringing the skis together.

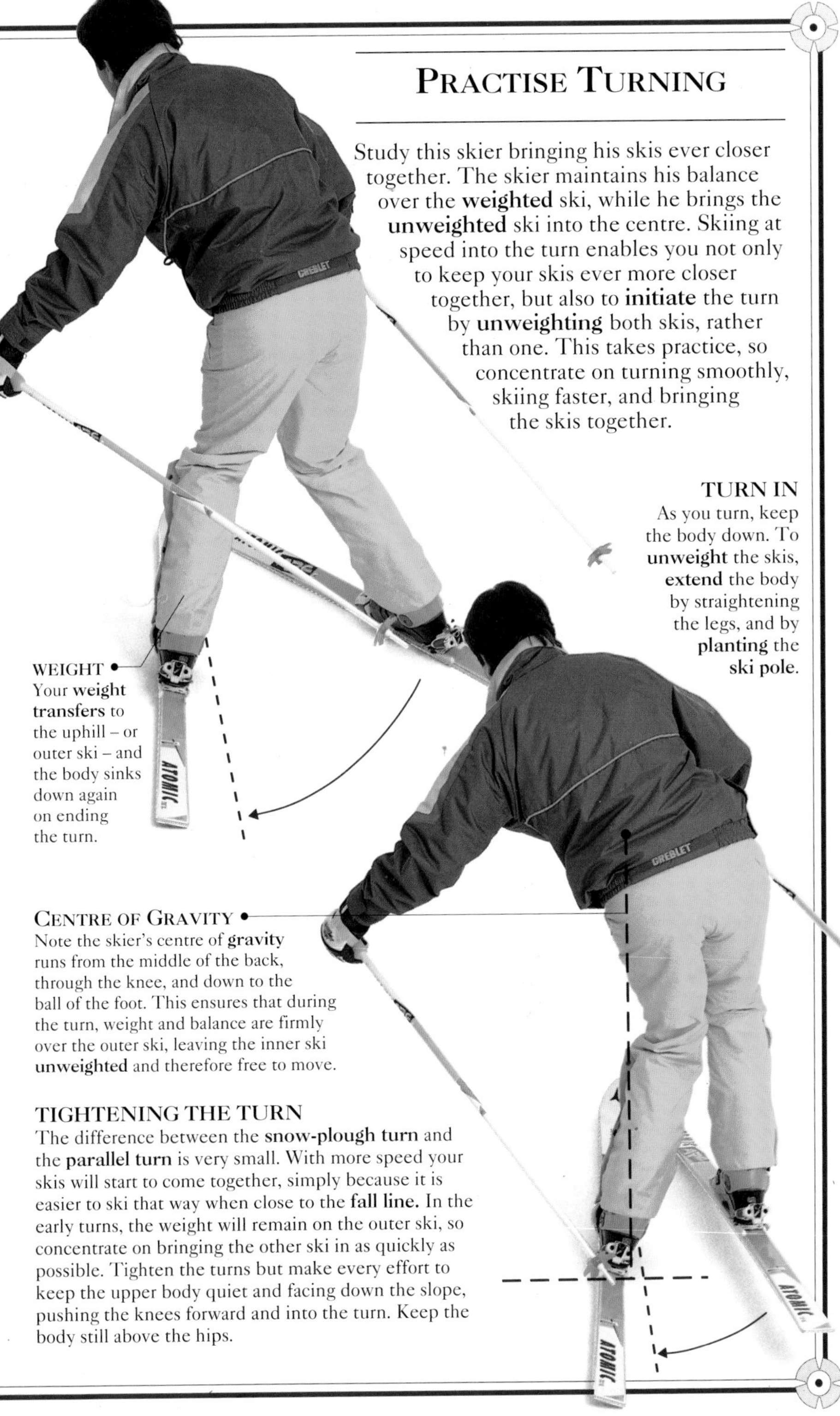

TURN IN
As you turn, keep the body down. To **unweight** the skis, **extend** the body by straightening the legs, and by **planting** the **ski pole**.

WEIGHT
Your **weight transfers** to the uphill – or outer ski – and the body sinks down again on ending the turn.

CENTRE OF GRAVITY
Note the skier's centre of **gravity** runs from the middle of the back, through the knee, and down to the ball of the foot. This ensures that during the turn, weight and balance are firmly over the outer ski, leaving the inner ski **unweighted** and therefore free to move.

TIGHTENING THE TURN
The difference between the **snow-plough turn** and the **parallel turn** is very small. With more speed your skis will start to come together, simply because it is easier to ski that way when close to the **fall line.** In the early turns, the weight will remain on the outer ski, so concentrate on bringing the other ski in as quickly as possible. Tighten the turns but make every effort to keep the upper body quiet and facing down the slope, pushing the knees forward and into the turn. Keep the body still above the hips.

IMPROVING BALANCE

Observe the skier (left): it may seem that he is sitting too far back and is totally out of balance, but in fact he is compensating for the speed and terrain as he travels directly down a bumpy slope. There is no one correct point of balance when skiing. You have to adjust your balance to the speed and terrain. Adjust your **open ski stance**, as needed, to keep in balance and under control. Balance and control go together – but balance comes first. If you get off balance you will soon be out of control.

DOWN A STEEP SLOPE
Keep the knees bent and forward when descending a steep slope. This helps keep pressure on the front of the skis, which provides most of the control. There is no need to have your skis tightly together, but keep them parallel.

ARMS
The arms act rather like wings, being important for maintaining lateral stability.

POSTURE
Adjust ski position to slope and terrain.

BODY
Relax the body forward over the knees and heels, but remaining able to **flex** up and down to absorb the bumps and stay in balance at all times.

POLES
Use **ski poles** to aid balance and control.

WEIGHT
Hold the weight now largely on the right ski, but **flex** both knees to provide fore and aft stability and to take out the effect of any bump.

SKIS
Keep the skis parallel and a hip's-width apart. If your weight is on the skis' **forebody**, they will not chatter on hard snow, and there is less danger that your **tips** will cross.

ALL-TERRAIN SKIING

Look at the skier (right) on soft snow, tackling a steep slope, yet he skis with confidence because he has learned the basic skills, and got them right long before skiing into this situation. He is balanced for the terrain, and skis smoothly, yet aggressively.

FLOWING LIKE A RIVER

GO WITH THE FLOW

Skiing is as much a mental as a physical exercise – a state of mind – so it helps to let your imagination work on a problem as a step towards solving it. For example, see the two skiers (left) descend a **mogul** field. When you find yourself in this situation, it helps to imagine how water flows down a rocky stream bed ... it does not dash itself against the stones but flows over the small stones, and glides round the large ones. Let the skis do the work, and avoid working them too hard with violent leg or upper body movements .

FRESH SNOW

Adapting to new, challenging conditions

NOT ALL YOUR SKIING will be on firm, groomed, or **pisted** snow. It can snow during your lesson or overnight, and the ability to cope with fresh snow is an essential skiing skill. Even fresh snow can vary – from the light and fluffy to the wet and heavy – but deep, fresh **powder** snow, offers the ultimate skiing experience, skiing **off-piste** through untracked snow. However, fresh snowfalls can be dangerous, so watch for the warning signs, the avalanche flags, the closed pistes. Don't be concerned if you can't see your skis, you shouldn't be looking at them anyway.

FEEL THE TURN

Skiing in fresh snow is a matter of balance. If you have good balance, then the skiing is actually easier; but you must make every effort to ski smoothly and keep your ski **tips** up. Stay close to the **fall line** and do not attempt wide turns. Extra speed helps you turn and, if you keep the ski tips up, your skis will **plane** over the snow.

• **ARMS**
Keep your arms well away from the body.

• **KNEES**
Use your knees to help steer your skis, turning them together.

• **LEGS**
Keep legs close, fluid, flexible, and together.

EASY FLUID MOVEMENT
This skier is staying close to the **fall line**, with her legs close together, and is banking into the turn. This is the ideal **powder snow** position, and completely secure. Deeper snow slows you down, so don't be afraid to point the skis directly down the slope. Keep skis together, and the **tips** of your skis up.

SKI TIPS FOR SKI TIPS

ANKLE-DEEP SNOW

Study the position of the skis in the snow and compare the two images. In ankle-deep snow, the skier can adopt the classic ski position and will find little resistance. His weight is balanced evenly down the centre of his skis, and the ski tips cut smoothly through the surface.

Skis rest on firm layer below ankle-deep snow.

KNEE-DEEP SNOW

The need to keep the ski tips up and breaking the surface of knee-deep snow requires a change of position and balance, as this skier reveals. Do not consciously sit back. Adjust your position just enough for the ski tips to break the surface and allow the ski to plane.

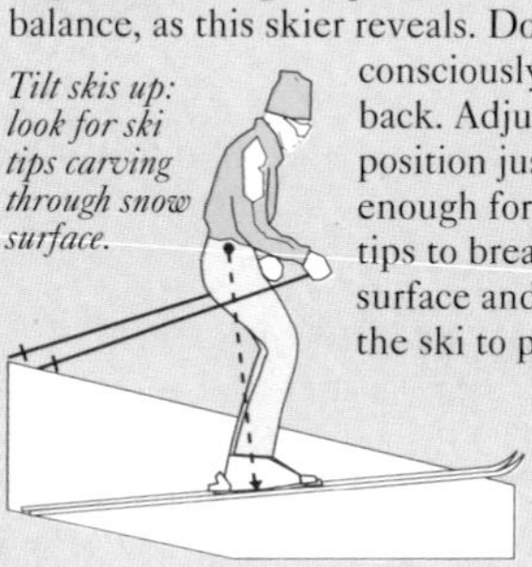

Tilt skis up: look for ski tips carving through snow surface.

ATTACKING THE SLOPE

Look forward, read the terrain and use speed to turn early and often

MOST BEGINNERS are afraid of speed, usually because they don't know how to control it. You must tackle this problem because to ski correctly you need some speed into the turn, and a certain amount of attack or aggression to get you round and heading in the required direction. Don't let your skis run away with you or slow down before the turn.

EYES
Look ahead and read the slope. Mark the spot where you are going to turn and remember that it is always best to turn early and turn often. Do not run out of slope.

GO FOR IT

You can't ski without turning, and speed helps you turn. Speed will also help you **unweight** the skis, and release you from the pull of **gravity**.

BODY RHYTHM
The good skier stays close to the fall line. Do likewise. The body is relaxed and forward, and one turn leads rhythmically into another.

LEGS
Bend the knees to keep the balance correct into the turn.

SPEED SAVES EFFORT

SPEED HELPS YOU TURN
Speed removes much of the physical effort from skiing, and enhances the movements that you have to make in order to turn or control the skis. In practice this means that just a small movement of the legs or body, plus a little speed, will give an effect equal to that of a large, unbalancing movement, executed at a slow speed.

Since speed saves effort, those who ski a little faster will become less tired and be able to ski better throughout the day. Another bonus from skiing faster is that to do so you have to ski better. Using speed when turning requires less **unweighting**, and leads to a quicker release and smoother execution of the turn, without the need for exaggerated movements and subsequent loss of posture and balance.

GET YOUR MIND IN GEAR

Visualize skiing the **fall line**, using speed, attacking the slope positively – just like this skier. Once you have mastered the basic skills, skiing is all in the mind. Believing you can do it, and doing it, is just a matter of confidence. That is the difference between this skier and yourself.

SENSE AND SAFETY

Following the ski code as well as the piste markers

SKIING IS A GREAT SPORT, but, as with all sports, accidents can happen. Observe the Ski Code: 1. Don't ski in a fashion that endangers others. 2. Ski to your own ability and to prevailing ground and weather conditions. 3. If coming from above or behind, choose your course to assure the security of the skier below or ahead. 4. Allow a wide margin when overtaking another skier. 5. Don't enter, cross, or start again after stopping on a piste, without checking for skiers. 6. Avoid stopping at narrow passages or in places with bad visibility. 7. If you are climbing, use only the side of the **piste**. If you are walking, avoid the centre of a piste and stay to one side. 8. Respect the signs on downhill pistes (see opposite).

WEATHERWATCH

DON'T THROW CAUTION TO THE WIND

Skiing takes place in the mountains, and mountain weather can be fickle, changing in minutes from clear, bright, and sunny, to a thick, freezing mist. It is worth remembering that at any time the temperature, high on a mountain, is normally lower than that in the valley, as the temperature drops an average of one degree centigrade for every hundred metres of ascent. You may not notice this in the sunshine, but you will notice it instantly if you move into shade or the sun goes behind a cloud. Bear this in mind every morning you set out skiing.

COMMON SENSE

Whatever the weather promises, allow for change. Take a sweater, a hat, an anorak. Beware of white-outs – a complete loss of visibility – and when you are in one, stay with your class and ski together. Never underestimate the mountains.

READING THE SIGNS

Pay attention to skiing information, dotted around the mountain slopes on boards and signs. These signs vary from informative to cautionary. Piste numbers, and small location, numbers (below), relate to the **piste map**.

BLUE RUN (EUROPE)
For skiers who have learned the basic techniques and need space. Blues have open slopes and room to turn without moguls, rocks, or trees. Green runs are even easier.

RED RUN (EUROPE)
For competent skiers, able to execute reliable parallel turns at some speed, reds contain a varied selection of difficulties as well as some open sections.

BLACK RUN (EUROPE)
Designed for expert skiers, black runs might have a virtually sheer wall, very narrow **piste,** lots of **moguls,** or be particularly tricky in poor conditions.

SIGNS AND TRAILS – USA
American resorts (as above) do not have "red" runs. The grades are "green"/beginners, "blue"/ intermediates, "black diamond"/more aggressive skier, and "double black diamond"/experts.

EUROPEAN SIGNS
Sign-codes for runs may vary, and differ from US.

DANGER SIGN •
If you see this sign watch out for **piste bashers,** pylons or other hazards.

Emergency telephone

Beware - piste basher

First-aid station

• AVALANCHE DANGER
Avalanches are not common, but the risk is always there, especially after heavy snow-falls. Never ski a closed run, marked by black-and-yellow chequered signs or flag.

FIRST AID AND TELEPHONES
Mark an injured skier's position by placing skis in a crossed upright position above the body. Get help by telephone or first-aid post.

GLOSSARY

A

• **Angulation** Position when *edging*, where the upper body leans out and the hips and knees are pushed into the slope. Also called the "comma".
• **Anticipation** Setting up body and skis, preparatory to *initiating* a turn.

B

• **Backward lean** To sit back slightly from standard skiing position to maintain balance or lift the *tips* of the skis out of soft snow.
• **Binding** Device with heel and toe-plate that attaches the boot to the ski, but releases under pressure.

C

• **Camber** Upward arch built into a ski to absorb the skier's weight, so that the *tip* and *tail* remains on the snow. Reverse camber is downward.
• **Carving** Turning on the *edges*, usually made at speed.
• **Catching an edge** To dig the side of the ski into the snow accidentally, which causes a fall.
• **Centre of gravity** The point of balance where the weight of the skier's body is concentrated.
• **Comma position** See Angulation.
• **Converging** Where the *tips* of the skis are closer together the *tails*.

D

• **Double pole push** To plant and push on both poles simultaneously to move forward, especialy on the flat.

E

• **Edges** Metal strips on either side of the ski base designed against wear and tear and as brakes.
• **Edging** Tilting the skis into the snow in order to provide the required amount of grip or bite.
• **Extension** Upward movement of the hips, knees, and ankles, to *unweight* the skis during a turn.

F

• **Fall line** The shortest and straightest line down any ski slope.
• **Flex** To adopt a low stance by bending the hips, knees, and ankles.
• **Forebody** Front section of the ski between the *tip* and the *waist*.
• **Forward lean** Leaning forward from the vertical to keep your weight on the *forebody*.

G

• **Gravity** The force that pulls a body towards the earth; the force by which skis run downhill.

H

• **Heel** The back part of the ski behind the waist – also called *tail*.

I

• **Initiation** The point at which the skier departs from his original line and begins the turn itself.

M

• **Mogul** A bump in the snow caused by the turning action of skis.

N

• **Nursery slope** Gentle slope for first-time skiers. Can be on upper slopes of a mountain, but usually close to ski school in the valley.

O

• **Off-piste** Ski slope not specially prepared nor sign-posted.
• **Open ski stance** Both skis a hip's-width apart in a parallel position.
• **Overturning** Turning too far into the hill after completing a turn.

P

- **Parallel turn** To change direction completely with skis parallel.
- **Piste** Prepared ski run, with groomed snow.
- **Piste basher** Large tracked vehicle with a snowplough on the front used for grooming snow slopes.
- **Piste map** Pocket layout of pistes and types of ski lifts.
- **Pole** – see *Ski poles*.
- **Pole plant** The point where the *ski pole* is set in the snow. Also the movement for doing this.
- **Powder snow** Light, often freshly fallen snow, which has not yet been compressed or pisted.
- **Preparation** The preliminary movement before initiating a turn, such as flexing the knees.

S

- **Schussing** Skiing a straight downhill run in the parallel position.
- **Side cut** Waisted shape of the ski which means that the ski is wider at the fore and aft than in the middle.
- **Side-slipping** Sliding sideways downhill under control.
- **Side-stepping** Climbing uphill sideways, one step at a time, usually on edged skis.
- **Skidding** When a ski slides, as opposed to carves, in a turn.
- **Ski poles** Support and balance poles, and aids in turning.
- **Sliding** When a ski glides forward or backward over snow.
- **Snow plough** Essential "V" shaped ski position, used for control.
- **Snow-plough turn** A turn *initiated* from the *snow plough* by the skier exerting more pressure, or body weight, on one ski.
- **Star turning** Turning on the spot by lifting the skis and pivoting in a circle on either the ski tips or tails.
- **Steering** The central part of a turn after the initiation.

T

- **Tail** The rear part of the ski.
- **Tip** The upward-curving front end of the ski. Also called the shovel.
- **Transfer your weight** see *Weight transfer*.
- **Traverse** To ski across the slope, at an angle to the *fall line*.

U

- **Unweighting** Extending the legs and body during a turn to reduce downward pressure on the turning skis and enable a turn to be executed with greater ease and speed.
- **Up extension** Unweighting the skis, throwing the body up by extending the knees and hips.

W

- **Waist** The central section of the ski that supports the binding.
- **Weighting** Exerting pressure on one ski to initiate or complete a turn.
- **Weight transfer** Shifting the weight from one ski to the other for stability or to start a turn.

INDEX

GETTING IN TOUCH

The Ski Club of Great Britain
118 Eaton Square
London SW1 W9AF
Tel. 071 245 1033.

British Ski Federation
258 Main Street, East Calder,
West Lothian EH53 OEE
Tel. 0506 88434.

ACKNOWLEDGMENTS

Konrad Bartelski, Robin Neillands and Dorling Kindersley would like to thank the following for their time, patience, and expertise in helping to prepare *Learn to Ski in a Weekend*:

Colin M.Callaghan (Managing Director) and Duncan R. Doak (Marketing) of Snowmec Leisure Environments, at Stafford Park, Telford, for the use of Snowmec's excellent and unique research and development snow refrigeration facility.
Katherine Foster for the additional ski modelling; Katherine, together with photographer Matthew Ward and his assistant, Martin Breschinski, endured the long photo-sessions at -10° C.
Louise Milburn at Lillywhites of Piccadilly Circus, London, for the loan of ski clothing and accessories on pp. 16-17.
Gary Smith at Watermead Slopes and Sails, Aylesbury, for the loan of the Poma lift on p. 15. Brian Thomas at Briton Engineering Developments Ltd., Netherton, Huddersfield, for the loan of the Doppelmayr T-bar on pp. 14-15.
Paul Bailey for the colour artwork on pp.70-71, Janos Marfy for the illustrations on pp. 19, 23, 90-91, and Peter Cooling for all the other illustrations.
Mark Shapiro (pp. 10-11, 82, 86), Stock Shot (pp. 2, 85 top, 89), Badger Sports (p. 87), Arthur Torr-Brown (pp. 12, 84, 85, 91), and *Outdoors Illustrated* (p. 12 top) for the use of location pictures.